HELPING THE THUMB-SUCKING CHILD

ROSEMARIE A. VAN NORMAN

AVERY PUBLISHING GROUP

Garden City Park • New York

The information and procedures contained in this book are based upon the research and the personal and professional experiences of the author, and should not be considered a replacement for consultation with a health-care professional. Should you have any questions regarding the information presented here, please discuss them with your health-care provider. It is a sign of wisdom, not cowardice, to seek a second or third opinion.

Cover Photograph: Photodisc
Cover design: Doug Brooks
Interior Illustrations: Dean Fritz
Typesetting: Gary Rosenberg & Helen Contoudis
Editor: Joan Taber Alteri

Avery Publishing Group
120 Old Broadway
Garden City Park, NY 11040
1–800–548–5757
www.averypublishing.com

Library of Congress Cataloging-in-Publication Data
Van Norman, Rosemarie.
    Helping the thumb-sucking child : a practical guide for
parents / Rosemarie Van Norman.
        p. cm.
    Includes bibliographical references and index.
    ISBN 0-89529-878-3
    1. Thumb sucking. 2. Thumb sucking—Prevention. I. Title.
HQ784.F5V35 1999   98-47201
649'.64—dc21   CIP

Printed in the United States of America.

10   9   8   7   6   5   4   3   2   1

CONTENTS

*This book is dedicated to the memory
of my father, Anthony James Weidner,
and my mother, Gladys Linnea Weidner,
for giving me life, love, and courage.*

ACKNOWLEDGMENTS

I want to extend my gratitude to many people for their support, shared learning experiences, and encouragement.

Preparation for this book began with my parents. They instilled in me a reverence for the innocence of children.

I thank Dr. Laren Teutsch for introducing me to the field of oral myology. This vocation has brought me immense gratification.

I am especially indebted to the many children and parents who allowed me to share in their private experiences with thumb-sucking behavior. This, in the end, provided effective techniques and supplied the concepts discussed in this work.

The idea of writing this book came from Dr. Marvin Hanson, a founding father of the International Association of Orofacial Myology, researcher, and retired Chairman of the Department of Communication Disorders at the University of Utah. He gave me the confidence I needed to accomplish this task, and then graciously evaluated my efforts throughout its development. To him I am particularly thankful.

I am deeply grateful to Dr. Robert Mason, Chief of Orthodontics at Duke University. For many years, Dr. Mason has contributed extensively to the development of appropriate philosophy in the treatment of oral-facial myofunctional disorders. When I requested his help with this project, he generously contributed an extraordinary amount of his time to gently prod, challenge, and guide me.

My sincere thanks go to Sheila Jones, Roberta Pierce, and Marjorie Schott, speech and language pathologists whose enthusiasm, support, and input over two decades brought into sharper focus the correlations between the sucking behavior and its impact on speech development and the learning process.

I am truly grateful to the many dental and medical professionals who allowed me to share in the care of their patients, and supported my treatment approach for the elimination of prolonged thumb- and finger-sucking habits.

I am deeply grateful to my cherished friends Marianne Lippincott, Sandie Rains, and Stan Teutsch for their love, confirmation, inspiration, and unending support. Without you, this dream would never have come to fruition.

A warm thanks is due to my family, especially my dear brother, Tony, who patiently rescued me from computer crashes innumerable times during my work on this book.

To my wonderful daughter and friend, Danielle—thank you for being so patient, understanding, and supportive while I was writing this book. I love you so much.

A special thanks to Rudy Shur and Avery Publishing Group for publishing this work, and to Joan Taber Altieri and Joanne Abrams for their enormous patience and talent.

Finally, for you, the reader, thank you for entrusting me with your time, and for reaching out for new ideas. This is testimony that you love your child and care about your relationship. It is my hope that this book will help you find positive courses of action that will benefit you and your child.

FOREWORD

In over thirty-five years of interactions with profession-als from a variety of dental, medical, and speech areas, I have never met anyone with more passion and dedi-cation to an idea, topic, or aspect of healthcare than Rosemarie Van Norman. You would have to meet Rose to experience the excitement in her eyes and voice when the topic of the elimination of thumb- and finger-sucking is discussed. This amazing woman has become the world's expert in this area by virtue of her tenacious study, clinical trials, and sustained concern for helping youngsters and others eliminate this troublesome habit.

I am delighted that Rose has decided to share her experi-ence, insight, and knowledge with the rest of us through this book. There is nothing like it anywhere else in profes-sional or popular literature. Her unique perspective repre-sents everything that should be said about thumb-sucking habits. In reading it, whether you are a parent or a profes-sional, you will like Rose as a person; you will respect her breadth of information; and you will learn from her descrip-tions of case studies from her professional practice.

Rose's method works because her techniques are based on sound principles of child development. No matter what the outcome, her goal is to enrich the self-image of her young patients. This is the best way of confronting the thumb-sucking habit. Indeed, it is certainly superior to trying to eliminate the habit with dental appliances, which treat the symptoms rather than the cause of the problem.

I commend this book to your reading and hope that you will share the joy and excitement that I experienced in learning more about this topic. Enjoy the awakening.

Robert M. Mason, Ph.D., D.M.D.
Speech and Language Pathologist, Dentist, Orthodontist
Professor and Chief of Orthodontics
Department of Surgery
Duke University Medical Center
Durham, North Carolina

PREFACE

I wrote this book because I have seen far too many preventable problems associated with prolonged thumb/finger-sucking, and I would like to offer a solution to parents and their children who are frustrated and despairing because they don't know how to correct the behavior.

I began working with youngsters with sucking habits twenty-six years ago in Dr. Laren Teutsch's pediatric dental practice. Dr. Teutsch was a wonderful, caring professional who truly embraced the concept of preventive dentistry. My employer's love for the human smile and his enthusiasm for his profession were strong and contagious. He was concerned about thumb-sucking because of the many dental problems they cause. Pressure applied during thumb-sucking can influence the position of teeth and bones in the upper and lower dental arches. If these oral structures don't form correctly, they can have a negative effect on a child's speech, ability to chew, and other functions.

We were introduced to the method of positive behavior modification for the elimination of thumb-sucking habits at an educational seminar run by Richard Barrett, a speech pathologist and pioneer in the field of oral myology—the study of oral-facial muscle function and its relationship to dental and speech development. Barrett was the first to develop and employ this method to help youngsters overcome sucking habits.

Dr. Teutsch was eager to offer Barrett's motivational approach to his patients with prolonged sucking habits. He asked me to set up a program that applied the basic concepts of positive behavior modification for the correction of thumb-sucking. It was, for me, the beginning of a lifelong passion.

Initially, I experienced reasonable success with the program. However, it didn't take long before I was perplexed! Although some of my patients had immediate and lasting success, others would slip back into their old habits after a few weeks or months. I found myself working with many children for months on end without helping them resolve their sucking behavior.

What was the problem? Why was this behavior so persistent in some children and not in others? Determined to find the answers, I began to search the available resources on the subject. I was already doing much of what the literature recommended—for example, using reminders, charts, and prizes as motivational tools—but solutions were not forthcoming. I concluded that the only way to learn about the causes and treatment of thumb-sucking was to conduct my own research as I continued studying the professional literature.

Little by little, through trial and error, patterns began to emerge. I discovered that habitual sucking is actually an extremely complex behavior. In addition, I learned that parents were having difficulty coping with the problem because the information available to them was confusing and inadequate. Some parents tried to ignore the behavior with the hope that it would stop when the child was "ready." Other parents unwittingly encouraged the habit by trying to eliminate it when the child was still too young. Both approaches can perpetuate the sucking behavior, often resulting in needless and preventable dental, speech, and emotional damage to the child.

There is hope! Over the years, the thousands of parents and children with whom I have worked have taught me a great deal. They have given me the clues to direct my search for solutions and to comprehend and unravel the mystery of this behavior. My motivational program to help youngsters eliminate their sucking habits has been highly successful. In fact, the vast majority of the children who have come to my office for help were able to overcome their sucking habits.

Although my role is important, I must give credit to the parents for helping these children resolve their sucking problems. They have been able to do so because they have made the effort to learn about the causes and treatment of thumb-sucking behavior, and in the process, they have acquired tools to understand and address the *whole* behavior through careful planning and active involvement.

Of course, sucking behavior is not restricted to the thumb. Sucking can involve any fingers; but because most infants and children prefer the thumb to the finger or fingers, I will refer to the behavior as thumb-sucking. This will avoid the repetition of thumb/finger-sucking throughout the book.

The purpose of this book is to share information about the nature of thumb-sucking and to teach parents about the most constructive, gentle, and effective techniques of habit elimination. You are about to learn about the many facets of the sucking activity, how it begins, and why it continues. You will learn about the role of the body's chemistry, as well as that of your child's intellectual growth and emotional development, and how they are related to sucking behaviors. Furthermore, you will discover which factors contribute to the persistence of thumb-sucking and what you can do to prevent it. Finally, you will be given logical, specific, step-by-step guidance and recommendations that work! Although there are many older youngsters, adolescents, and adults with sucking habits, the treatment program described in this book is directed toward five-year-olds. Nevertheless, the basic concepts of treatment involve effective techniques to eliminate sucking habits in any age group. In addition, a list of suggested readings found in the back of this book presents some excellent books that offer help in solving some of the problems associated with prolonged thumb-sucking.

This book is not meant to instill anxiety or guilt in parents. However, you may not realize that your child has a problem in the area of dental, speech, physical, or emotional development that has been caused by the sucking habit. And it is likely that you haven't been made aware of the direct relationship between these problems and thumb-sucking. This book will help you recognize and understand that relationship. My treatment techniques will give you a new way to work with your child at an appropriate time, in a confident, sensible, compassionate, and positive way.

Rosemarie Van Norman
Omaha, Nebraska

A WORD ABOUT GENDER

Your child is certainly as likely to be a girl as a boy. However, our language does not provide us with a genderless pronoun. To avoid using the awkward "he/she" or the impersonal "it" when referring to your child, while still giving equal time to both sexes, the feminine pronouns "she," "her," and "hers" have been used in odd-numbered chapters, while the male "he," "him," and "his" appear in all the rest. This decision was made in the interest of simplicity and clarity.

INTRODUCTION

John and Cindy were attending a Christmas play at their daughter's elementary school. Seven-year-old Susie was playing the part of an angel. As they heard the parents around them snickering about the angel sucking her thumb on stage in front of the entire audience, John and Cindy cringed with embarrassment. The angel was their little Susie! Was this an isolated, rare incident? Not at all. It is very likely that similar scenarios occur routinely at most elementary schools.

Over the past twenty-six years, I have received thousands of calls from frustrated parents who don't know what to do about their thumb-sucking children. Their comments are fairly standard: "We've tried everything to stop the behavior and nothing works; my child is sucking now more than ever! When will my son be ready to stop the sucking habit? Should I ignore it? Should I spank or try to reason with my daughter? Will the sucking habit affect my child's dental or speech development? If I try to get my child to stop sucking, will the youngster be psychologically traumatized or begin some other aberrant behavior?"

Parents are concerned about their children's self-esteem because of negative remarks about the sucking activity from peers, siblings, and other relatives. Their concern can even put a strain on their marital relationship. They wonder if their child needs the sucking activity because of emotional insecurity; or they wonder if they have done something wrong as parents.

Thumb-sucking is very common in infants and toddlers. In fact, parents are often surprised to learn that 75 to 95 percent of infants in western cultures engage in *non-nutritive* sucking—the sucking of thumb, fingers, and pacifiers. Many children stop this normal behavior with little or no intervention by their parents. But many do not stop, and appropriate help is often difficult to find.

How prevalent is prolonged sucking behavior—non-nutritive sucking beyond the age of five? No one knows how widespread the activity is because it is often done in secret, surrounded by embarrassment and shame. The most comprehensive survey of the incidence of thumb-sucking habits was conducted between 1963 and 1965 by the United States Division of Health Examination Statistics. The study included approximately 8,000 children between the ages of six and eleven. Researchers estimated that 10 percent of American children in this age group—about 2.4 million youngsters—have active thumb-sucking habits. Another study, published in the *Journal of Dentistry for Children* in 1976, reported that 19 percent of children in the United States continue the behavior after age five. And in 1994 speech pathologists who had conducted a study of 371 American children between the ages of six and nine found that 26 percent of them had active thumb-sucking habits. One thing is certain—there are *millions* of individuals with prolonged thumb-sucking habits.

Most parents receive lots of varied and conflicting advice from family, friends, and health professionals. They are advised either to encourage their child to eliminate the habit immediately or to ignore it entirely. In the latter case, they are assured that peer pressure will force the youngster to stop thumb-sucking when he enters kindergarten.

Many parents wait and wait and wait for their child to stop the sucking activity. And when the behavior doesn't stop, they become frustrated. They may try to eliminate the habit before the youngster is capable of understanding why thumb-sucking is a problem or before he is capable of practicing self-control. Parents may begin to employ methods of habit elimination before they understand the biological, physiological, or psychological cues that stimulate their child's sucking activity. And although their intentions are good, their efforts often entrench the very habit they are trying to eliminate. The result is that parents and children end up feeling anxious, annoyed, and helpless.

Sucking habits have different psychological significance for different age groups. Parents should *not* be concerned about their infant or toddler who sucks a thumb or finger. However, a five-year-old who continues frequent sucking activity is cause for concern for a number of reasons. Sucking habits can have a negative impact on speech and on dental and emotional growth and development. Fortunately, many of these problems can be diminished or eliminated with early intervention. But the longer the sucking habit is present, the more difficult it is to overcome. This is because sucking is a stress reliever, and children become emotionally dependent on sucking for solace and comfort. This does not mean that the child is emotionally insecure or that the parents are to blame. In fact, most of the children I have treated come from loving, caring families. We must view the stress factors from a child's perspective. Normal events, such as the arrival of a new sibling or starting a new school, can stimulate an increase in the sucking activity. Without a doubt, life becomes more complex and stressful with age, and, so the child's dependence on the sucking activity becomes more profound.

There are biological, chemical, and psychological elements to this behavior. Understanding the combination of body chemistry and psychological circumstances is crucial to effective correction of prolonged sucking habits. These elements will be discussed in the chapters ahead.

Chapter 1 through Chapter 4 will help you understand the sucking behavior, how some children pick up the habit, and the role played by the brain in perpetuating the habit. You will learn about many of the problems created by the sucking behavior and how family, friends, and teachers can help or hurt the thumb-sucking child. Some descriptions of the dental problems associated with thumb-sucking are accompanied by photographs. In some instances, psychological problems and social problems are personalized by case histories of thumb-sucking children.

Chapter 5 through Chapter 9 will guide you in helping your child overcome the sucking habit. You will learn how to evaluate the severity of your child's habit, how to react to it, and how to plan for its elimination in the most responsible and effective way possible. More important, you will find out how to help your child maintain successful elimination by learning when and how to ease up on behavior modification methods and by learning about the many enjoyable things you can do with your child to distract him from the thumb-sucking activity.

Helping the Thumb-Sucking Child will provide you with the tools you need to work with your child to overcome behavior that can cause all sorts of problems, from crooked teeth and speech problems to feelings of unworthiness to ostracism by other children. The result will be a much happier and healthier child, a less stressful family situation, and an enriched parent-child relationship. The rewards for you, your child, and your family will last a lifetime.

Chapter 1

UNDERSTANDING THE CAUSES OF THUMB-SUCKING

The infant's sucking instinct is essential for survival. Through the use of ultrasound, we know that many fetuses suck their thumbs and fingers in utero; and some even arrive in the delivery room with fully developed calluses on their thumbs, fingers, wrists, and hands. But why do infants begin sucking their thumbs and fingers after birth? Many studies have found that habitual thumb-sucking is rare in cultures where infants have constant access to their mothers' breasts. For example, in the tribal society of the !Kung Sans, who live in the Kalahari desert, mothers carry their infants in a sling throughout the day, and they bring them to bed with them at night. The mothers' breasts are usually bare, so the infants can easily suckle whenever they want to. The researchers conclude that this allows for complete satisfaction of the infant's sucking urge and, consequently, !Kung babies have no need to suck their thumbs. But infants in the industrialized world are not always given the same opportunity to suckle whenever they want, which may be one way to explain why many of them suck the thumb, finger, or a pacifier.

In this chapter, we will explore some of the physical and psychological reasons that babies begin the activity, and we will see why some children continue it long after their peers have stopped.

WHY DOES THUMB-SUCKING BEGIN?

Sucking anything for purposes other than food or nutrition is called *non-nutritive* sucking. As we mentioned, many infants suck in utero and continue to do so immediately after birth whenever they manage to get their fingers to their mouth. Sometimes, it takes a little longer for babies to begin the thumb-sucking activity because they are not yet coordinated enough to bring their thumb up to their mouth at will. But at around three months, babies discover their hands; and they play with them continually, holding one hand with the other; opening and closing them, and, of course, tasting them. The exploration begins! From this point, everything the infant can grasp goes directly to her mouth for entertainment, contemplation, and discovery. Sucking fixations and oral fixations in infants provide stimulation that is essential for the development of the central nervous systems. These are normal behaviors that teach babies to discern things such as temperature, texture, color, shape, size, and proximity.

During this time of exploration, many infants discover that sucking their thumb is a pleasure similar to that of sucking a bottle or mother's breast. They seem to regard their thumb as an extension of their mother and the feeding experience. Whenever they want, they can enjoy the soothing sense of gratification that comes from sucking, because their thumb is always with them, and their maturing motor functions allow easy accessibility. The behavior eventually becomes automatic—the babies are sucking their thumbs without being aware that they are doing it.

While many infants suck their thumbs, others do not. And some children don't begin the behavior until well after infancy. In order to understand why some children begin thumb-sucking, it will be helpful to learn about some of its benefits as well as some of the factors that may encourage the behavior.

The Benefits of Thumb-Sucking

Thumb-sucking can help infants adjust to their new world. Before birth, the mother's body provides all the fetus's in-utero needs. It is kept warm, fed, comfortable, and protected. Upon arrival into the world, the changes are dramatic. The infant is suddenly exposed to a barrage of random stimuli such as cold, hunger, light, darkness, and noise. All these changes are startling, and they can overload the newborn's nervous system. The result is a crying, distressed baby. The activity of thumb-sucking allows infants to gain a sense of control, to calm and soothe themselves, and to shut out undesired stimuli. This soothing, calming effect helps them fall asleep; and it aids digestion, breathing, and heart rate. Hence, thumb-sucking babies can be a joy to care for because they feel safe and comfortable. They eat well, sleep well, and tend to be content and easy-going.

Gender Differences

Thumb-sucking behavior appears to be more prevalent in girls than in boys. In my data on 723 individuals with prolonged sucking habits, 489 were females and 234 were males. In fact, a number of surveys conducted between 1962 and 1994 determined that prolonged sucking habits are more common in girls than in boys and that girls stick with the behavior longer than boys do. No one knows why this is, but some believe it is because as boys grow and develop, they tend to be more active than girls, and thus have less inclination to thumb-suck.

Mimicking and Thumb-Sucking

It is said that imitation is the sincerest form of flattery. The behavior begins very early in babies, and then continues throughout childhood and adolescence. Infants and toddlers are like little sponges, absorbing everything they see. They mimic the actions of the people around them, which makes them feel that they belong, encourages communication, and teaches them new skills. Young children not only imitate their parents, they imitate the behavior of their playmates and other children around them. And this can lead them to adopt thumb-sucking behavior.

> Maura mimicked my daughter Danielle's attachment to her blanket. The girls had met each other when they were about three years old and quickly became best friends. Danielle had two identical "blankies"—this spared her the trauma of separation when one was in the wash—that she carried with her everywhere. She had a habit of curling her blanket around the bridge of her nose and rubbing it gently while she sucked her fingers. Evidently, Maura thought that the blanket deal was pretty neat, so she found a special blanket of her own. But Maura had misinterpreted what Danielle was doing with her blanket near her nose. So instead of rubbing the blanket, she would stuff a corner of it into her nose! In time, Maura became very attached to her blanket, and

would become distressed when her mother took it away to wash it. She didn't care how smelly it had gotten—she liked the way it smelled! Much to her parents' chagrin, long after Danielle had given up her blankies, Maura was still mesmerized by her ratty old blanket and the pleasure she got from stuffing it up her nose.

Thumb-sucking often begins when a child imitates another child who has a sucking habit. Because many preschoolers have sucking habits, and millions of these children attend daycare facilities, it is easy to understand how other youngsters may begin the behavior through imitation. Indeed, thumb-sucking is not confined to toddlers in daycare centers. Even children in the early elementary grades may begin sucking by mimicking another child at school. One first-grader with highly developed social skills was referred to me by her teacher because many of her classmates were copying her thumb-sucking. They were not making fun of her—she was highly valued as a friend, and their sucking was a demonstration of kinship! But the teacher found this conduct in so many of her students to be less than conducive to the learning process.

It is not unusual to find several youngsters in one family with thumb-sucking habits that are a direct result of one child imitating another. Children will often start the sucking activity when a new baby arrives in the family. The behavior may be stimulated by the older child's desire to receive the same amount of attention being given to the newborn. The child may initiate sucking on the baby's bottle or pacifier, or by imitating the baby's thumb-sucking behavior. Sometimes, the reverse can happen. Toddlers, who adore their older siblings, often follow them around like shadows and imitate their every behavior. If an older sibling happens to have a sucking habit, the toddler will sometimes demonstrate her affection for a sibling by imitating the sucking habit—even choosing the same thumb on the same hand!

Pacifier Use

It is a common misconception that children who suck pacifiers will rarely suck their thumb or that the use of a pacifier will prevent thumb-sucking. According to data I have collected on 723 children I treated for prolonged thumb-sucking habits, 243, or 34 percent, began habitual sucking behavior on a pacifier. Their parents reported that these children had initially sucked only on a pacifier, not on a pacifier and a thumb. When infants who had become used to a pacifier developed the motor skills to bring their thumbs to their mouths at will, they would suck their thumbs whenever the pacifier wasn't available. After all, the thumb is much handier! The same thing can happen to pacifier-sucking toddlers whose parents suddenly decide to eliminate the pacifier from their child's life—their thumb becomes a substitute for the missing pacifier. They may also begin sucking on their tongue, lip, blanket, or other objects when the pacifier is taken away. If your child uses a pacifier, *gradually* limit its use; and, certainly, try to avoid overusing it as a convenience.

WHY MIGHT THUMB-SUCKING CONTINUE?

We now understand that some babies thumb-suck in utero and that the behavior may continue throughout infancy. And we have seen that children may acquire sucking habits as a result of mimicking other children or using a pacifier. But why does the behavior continue—often far into childhood? To understand this, it will be helpful to learn a few basics about the chemistry of the brain.

We now know that the brain has the ability to manufacture its own mood-altering chemicals. The brain has billions of nerve cells that communicate with one another through *neurotransmission*—the sending of nerve impulses from one part of the body to another. Neurotransmission stimulates the brain to produce certain chemicals and thus controls all emotions, perceptions, and bodily functions.

Harvey Milkman and Stanley Sunderwirth, who co-authored the book *Craving for Ecstasy: The Consciousness and Chemistry of Escape,* remark that the discovery of the central nervous system's ability to produce its own narcotics has led to a re-examination of the biological, chemical, and psychological reasons for many compulsive behaviors. Pleasurable activities such as jogging, gambling, sex, eating, and *thumb-sucking* stimulate the brain to produce these chemicals. In order to prevent or eliminate habitual thumb-sucking behavior, it is crucial that we understand what triggers the activity. In other words, we must understand its physical and psychological "cues."

Increased and Decreased Neurotransmission

The body uses two types of neurotransmissions—*increased* and *decreased* neurotransmission. As these terms imply, each has a different effect on the body.

Increased neurotransmission produces feelings of excitement or arousal. Individuals who enjoy activities that produce these sensations often become inclined toward risk-taking activities.

Decreased neurotransmission produces a calming, relaxing sensation. Thumb-sucking causes this type of neurotransmission. As the child sucks, the brain produces chemicals called *enkephalins* and related compounds called *endorphins,* which decrease neurotransmission. These compounds are the body's opiates or analgesics. They reduce feelings of discomfort and pain, and they create a feeling of euphoria—a deep sense of well-being—much like that produced by drugs such as opium. The neuronal pathways associated with pain pass through the portion of the brain known as the *limbic system,* which is the center of emotions and feelings. This is the reason that substances with pain-reducing properties have a tranquilizing effect on the emotions.

Another way to understand the effect of decreased neurotransmission is to think of the relaxed, sleepy sensation we experience after eating a big meal. Eating enjoyable food results in decreased neurotransmission and the release of endorphins, which has a mood-calming effect. Milkman and Sunderwirth contend that this might explain why some individuals turn to food in order to reduce their emotional stress. Eating results in decreased neurotransmission, discharge of the body's endorphins, and therefore the mood-calming end result. Thumb-sucking triggers the same physical and psychological process.

Sucking, Pleasure, and Biology

The infant's first association with pleasure and a soothing, calming sensation is the act of sucking and eating. The first food is milk, which also decreases neurotransmission. Modern brain chemistry studies substantiate the old folklore that drinking warm milk helps people relax and fall asleep. This is because milk contains the amino acid *tryptophan.* The body converts this amino acid into *serotonin,* which decreases neurotransmission and produces a tranquilizing effect on the central nervous system.

In short, sucking and warm milk cause decreased neurotransmission, which leads to the production of endorphins, which creates sensations of pleasure, comfort, and relaxation. The infant quickly makes the connection. Thus, it is not hard to understand why thumb or pacifier sucking is associated with pleasure, self-gratification, and comfort.

Why Parents' Methods May Fail

As most babies develop, increase physical mobility, and gain independence, they stop the thumb-sucking behavior on their own with little or no interference by their parents. But some youngsters continue to thumb-suck. And parents sometimes decide to take measures to eliminate their child's thumb-sucking before they understand the physical and emotional cues that trigger it. As a result, they inadvertently entrench the habit. Then, in their frustration, parents may actually begin to scold or punish their child for sucking on her thumb, which only complicates matters. How? By creating anxiety and physical discomfort in the child—the very cues that cause children to indulge in thumb-sucking. This situation stimulates the desire for the relief produced by the sucking behavior, and the child sucks even more.

CONCLUSION

Clearly, thumb-sucking is far more involved than it appears to be. It is much more complex than a simple physical act. It involves neurotransmission, the production of mood-altering chemicals, physical and psychological dependence, and a behavior that is often habitual. In addition, thumb-sucking is frequently complicated by well-intentioned, but often destructive, tactics aimed at its elimination. In the following chapter, we will see that if the thumb-sucking habit persists, it can also place the emotional health of the child at risk.

Chapter 2

PROLONGED SUCKING HABITS AND SOCIAL INTERACTION

When I began working with youngsters with sucking habits, I was primarily concerned with dental and speech problems associated with the behavior. Physical problems such as these can generally be fixed; but, the psychological problems associated with prolonged thumb-sucking are not easily remedied. Many youngsters with sucking habits experience significant emotional trauma because parents, siblings, relatives, peers, teachers, daycare providers, and, at times, even total strangers make them feel ashamed of their thumb-sucking behavior. The result is a child with low self-esteem—a child who places little value on himself. Multiple trauma and insults to an innocent child can do enormous damage. Children who are constantly under pressure to stop sucking their thumb begin to regard themselves as bad children with nothing good to offer. In time, they can become withdrawn, anxious, angry, or aggressive.

In this chapter, we will talk about the importance of family, peers, and teachers in the development of self-esteem in children; and we will hear the stories of three youngsters whose prolonged sucking habits were directly influenced by their feelings of worthlessness.

HOW MIGHT THE FAMILY FOSTER PROLONGED THUMB-SUCKING?

The family's influence during a child's early years determines how he will respond to life's ups and downs in the years to come. It is during this period that children develop self-esteem, which will have a major effect on their success in life. Volumes of research have shown that many people in a child's environment play a crucial role in the development of his self-esteem, but the family is the first great influence. Children are extremely vulnerable emotionally, especially before the age of eight. During this time, they rely on their parents' reactions to know if they are valued. All children experience occasional rejection or negative responses from other people, but if they can depend on their parents to assure them that they are loved and cherished, it is not inevitable that their self-esteem will suffer lasting damage.

Naturally, parents want their children to feel safe, happy, and loved; but sometimes they inadvertently send a different message to them. For instance, if parents argue with one another—especially about their child's thumb-sucking behavior—it sends a message to the child that he is not quite so special in the eyes of his parents. Making matters worse, it is not uncommon for the youngster to blame himself for the conflict.

When Parents Don't Agree

I have never encountered parents who didn't love their children or want the best for them. But parents don't always agree with each other about child-rearing practices; or they can have completely different personalities. For example, one parent may feel that a child's sucking activity is not an issue, while the other is extremely annoyed by it. Or perhaps one parent is permissive and the other is a disciplinarian, or one is relaxed and the other is intense and highly structured. Unfortunately, these differences can result in conflict. If the child feels at fault for his parents' arguing, it can only exacerbate a thumb-sucking habit.

> Jeff was nine years old when he was referred to me by his speech therapist. He had been in therapy for two years trying to correct a lisp—substituting the *th*-sound for the *s*-sound. Jeff had extremely crooked teeth as well as a bite problem as a result of his thumb-sucking habit. For this reason, his lisp persisted and he was not being helped by speech therapy.
>
> Jeff's mother told me that she and her husband had been trying to eliminate Jeff's sucking habit for years! His pediatrician, dentist, and orthodontist had told her to ignore it, that he would stop thumb-sucking when he was ready. The problem was compounded because his father, who was extremely authoritarian, expected Jeff to stop thumb-sucking simply because he told him to stop. And he often disciplined Jeff by humiliating him, denying privileges, or banishing him to his room. Although Jeff's father loved him, he was concerned about his son's dental and speech problems, and he didn't know what to do. He began to criticize Jeff's mother for being negligent. She was the parent who was with Jeff most of the time, and she should have been able to control Jeff's sucking activity.
>
> His parents' arguments over his sucking behavior provoked even more thumb-sucking. Jeff

felt unable to control the activity. He became withdrawn, spending much of his time alone in his room to avoid hearing his parents argue.

Counseling enabled his parents to see that their arguments were causing Jeff to suck even more. They began to change their attitudes and their behavior, which ultimately helped Jeff overcome his habit. He was immensely proud of his accomplishment. His father later told me that the experience had been a real education for him— one that had enriched his relationship with his wife, his son, and his entire family.

Clearly, it is important that any existing parental conflict is resolved. Often, this eliminates the major source of stress and self-blame from children's lives, giving them less reason to turn to their thumbs for solace.

The Important Role of Siblings

Siblings can have a great impact on one another. In fact, an older sibling can have as much influence as a parent can. An older brother or sister may be embarrassed by a younger sibling's thumb-sucking, particularly if the youngster with the habit is over the age of five or six. Even the most loving sibling might scold a younger child for sucking his thumb, and this can be extremely upsetting for the youngster. And we now know that when a thumb-sucking child is upset, it only increases the sucking behavior.

A certain amount of sibling rivalry is normal in children who are relatively close in age, and sometimes one child will make fun of the other for thumb-sucking. As long as this isn't ongoing and as long as the child isn't taking his cue from the parents, the thumb-sucking sibling won't feel emotionally battered. But sometimes parents may inadvertently favor a non-thumb-sucking child over a sibling who does thumb-suck. This favoritism can lead to severe cases of rivalry; and it can potentially damage the emotional well-being of the thumb-sucking youngster, causing the child to suck more and more. It is important for parents to make sure that sibling rivalry is not exacerbating a sucking habit.

When siblings are treated equally by their parents, they often become allies. In fact, I have seen cases in which siblings actually helped their brother or sister overcome prolonged thumb-sucking. And in these cases, all the family members benefited.

The Important Role of Grandparents

It might be surprising to know that grandparents can have a big impact on their grandchild's life—even if their visits are only occasional. Their love and understanding can help a child thrive, or their constant criticism can make him feel inept. They can even influence their grandchild's sucking behavior.

Many grandparents have great difficulty coping with a grandchild's sucking habit. Some are concerned about other children making fun of the child, and others believe the behavior is an indication of emotional insecurity. They may think the thumb-sucking activity reflects a problem with their own parenting skills or those of their children. Whatever their attitude, children will pick up on it and react to it—especially if the attitude is negative. Some parents have even told me that their child starts sucking whenever the grandparents come to visit! If grandparents are constantly critical of their grandchild's thumb-sucking, the child may begin to associate the grandparents' arrival with criticism of the sucking behavior and with feelings of anxiety. And this makes them suck all the more.

WHAT HAPPENS WHEN SUCKING
HABITS CONTINUE AT SCHOOL?

The family's influence certainly doesn't stop once the child starts to go to school, for it has laid the foundation for the school experience. But, as we will see, schoolmates and teachers play an extremely important role in a child's life. Their power to help or hurt a youngster is even stronger when the youngster enters school with a sucking habit; and if he carries the thumb-sucking activity into the classroom, the results can be disastrous.

Many people believe that their children will stop sucking behaviors as soon as they enter school because the pressure from other children will be so great. This view suggests that rejection and ostracism by peers is a *good* way to eliminate the sucking habit. As we have learned, negative reactions from other people create stress and feelings of inadequacy in a child with habitual sucking behavior; and this tends to trigger, rather than discourage, the activity. Furthermore, even though many children will not suck in the classroom, this does not mean that they have eliminated the habit. They often resume the behavior as soon as the school day is over.

How Learning and Socializing
Are Affected by Thumb-Sucking

By now, we are aware of the tremendous impact the family can have on all aspects of a child's life—not only on a child's sucking behavior, but on how that child functions in the school setting. School is a child's second home. And just as children want to be accepted by their parents and siblings, they want to be to be accepted by their teachers and their peers. Children who are rejected by their peers don't have the opportunity to interact socially. Therefore, it is almost impossible for them to learn the appropriate social skills that are so important to the development of emotionally healthy children.

An article published in *Clinical Pediatrics*, "Thumb-Sucking: Pediatricians' Guidelines," by Friman and Schmidt concludes that parents should help their children eliminate a thumb-sucking habit *before* they begin elementary school so that they won't be ostracized by classmates. The authors found that first-graders generally think that children who thumb-suck are less attractive and not as likeable as their non-thumb-sucking peers. Children can be cruel and brutally frank. Any noticeable difference such as freckles, glasses, or a speech impediment can provoke unkind treatment. A child with a sucking habit is very likely to be rejected by his classmates. Furthermore, constant thumb sucking interferes with the development of communication skills, and it can create many speech-related problems. Obviously, this impairs a child's ability to interact socially. Many parents observe that their child is much more verbal both at home and at school once his thumb-sucking behavior has been overcome.

In addition to problems with classmates, children who thumb-suck in the classroom may have difficulty concentrating on their subjects. Writing, manipulative skills, and general class participation can be limited by the activity. This often irritates teachers who don't understand the problems that trigger the behavior.

The Teacher's Role in Perpetuating or Stopping Thumb-Sucking

Although most teachers are accepting and tolerant of students with sucking habits, parents are justifiably concerned about the negative reactions of some teachers to thumb-sucking in the classroom. A critical teacher can be a real problem for a youngster with a sucking habit.

The mother of one of my patients broke down in tears because of the way her seven-year-old's teacher was dealing with her daughter's sucking behavior.

> Sandra's teacher viewed thumb-sucking as a character flaw and refused to tolerate it in her classroom. She would often make comments about the sucking activity in front of the child's classmates, and they would join in and ridicule her about the habit.
>
> Sandra was going through a difficult adjustment at home. The family's recent move to a new town had coincided with the birth of a baby and a new school for Sandra. These events were overwhelming for the youngster, which of course stimulated an increase in her sucking activity. When I began working with Sandra, I evaluated the circumstances that were contributing to the sucking behavior and discussed them with her parents. We decided that the best way to help Sandra would be to give her total reprieve from any attention to the sucking behavior for the time being. This would give her an opportunity to adjust to all the changes in her life. Her teacher was given pertinent information about the causes and treatment of thumb-sucking and was asked to go along with this plan. Once Sandra's parents and teacher understood what was triggering Sandra's sucking activity, they were able to help her by giving her the support and encouragement she needed to eliminate the habit. Her mother reported that the teacher had made a ninety-degree turnaround and had been very supportive once she had a better understanding of the sucking behavior.

Other Habits in the School Setting

Another very important reason to help your child elimi-nate sucking behavior before he enters elementary school is that children who are making an effort to avoid sucking behavior at school sometimes pick up other habits *in ad-dition to* their thumb-sucking. For example, approximately 30 percent of the children I treat for prolonged thumb-sucking have fingernail-biting habits! Many youngsters who try not to thumb-suck in the classroom begin to chew on their fingernails, clothing, hair, pencils, and other objects. Subsequently, they end up with *two* oral habits— sucking and chewing.

Some children who are trying to control a sucking habit in the classroom may become agitated and have difficulty sitting still. And their exasperation sometimes leads to dis-ruptive and combative behavior. When these emotional problems are combined with some of the physical conse-quences of thumb-sucking, such as protruding teeth, school life can become a nightmare for a child. In such cases, his self-esteem is so low, it becomes impossible for him to overcome the thumb-sucking behavior without help.

Mary Lou was a nine-year-old referred to me by her speech pathologist. Her sucking habit had caused her front teeth to protrude, which had contributed to a serious lisping problem. Mary Lou had recently transferred from a private school to a public school because she had been doing poor-ly in her schoolwork. Her classmates continually ridiculed her because of her thumb-sucking and her distorted speech. Of course, her emotional pain stimulated even more sucking activity at school, which only intensified the ostracism.

Mary Lou's new teacher was concerned because of the thumb-sucking, which she felt was having a negative influence on her ability to concentrate. And it was certainly preventing her from having a healthy relationship with her new classmates.

Mary Lou had a beautiful, creamy complexion, lovely blue eyes, and naturally wavy auburn hair; but the severe protrusion of her upper front teeth was a real distraction. When she was six years old, her dentist had given her a removable appliance for her mouth to serve as a reminder not to suck and to correct some of her dental problems. But the timing had been extremely poor because she was just starting first grade, which is a stressful time for many youngsters. In addition, she was coping with the arrival of a new baby in the family. She removed the dental appliance and continued sucking. Her parents were frustrated, and Mary Lou felt like a failure.

When the child came to me for the first appointment, she held her head down, afraid to make eye contact. I assured her that I was there to help her. With her eager cooperation, we started a program of positive behavior modification; and, with the informed, positive, and focused support of her parents, she conquered her habit. Her success gave her a tremendous boost in self-esteem.

When Mary Lou came back for her six-month visit, her eyes sparkled and it was clear that she was feeling good about herself! Her father told me she was a different person—she had made many friends, and she was feeling confident about herself. And she had brought her grades from failing to above average. Her teacher confirmed that the elimination of the habit had made a profound impact on her scholastic performance and her social life at school.

CONCLUSION

There is no doubt that prolonged sucking habits can hurt children's self-esteem because of the way the people around them react to them. In turn, their social development can't proceed at a normal level and pace because they don't feel worthy of interacting with their peers. A devastating pattern of behavior is developed, which can follow a child into adulthood. Mary Lou's dental problems were severe; but, in comparison to the emotional trauma she had endured, they were minor.

The older the child is, the more difficult it is to overcome a sucking habit. As a child grows and life becomes more complex, his emotional dependence on thumb-sucking becomes much more profound. And, as we have seen in this chapter, pressure from family members, teachers, and peers only increases sucking behavior.

If children can be helped to eliminate their sucking behavior at about the age of five, before they start kindergarten, many problems will be avoided. Nevertheless, careful planning is essential—the right time must be picked before addressing the habit. Particular consideration must be given to the child's intellectual and emotional development and to stress factors from the child's perspective. We will explore these important issues in greater detail in later chapters.

Chapter 3

DENTAL AND SPEECH DEVELOPMENT IN THUMB-SUCKING CHILDREN

All systems of the body are linked together so that each part has a functional relationship with another part. Form and function are reciprocal. This means that if there is a malformation of the mouth or if the teeth are not properly aligned, the musculature of the tongue, lips, and cheeks must compensate in order to adapt to the deformity. Simply put, if they do not adapt, there will be problems with their ability to function. Of course, a major function of the oral cavity is speech production. When children thumb-suck over a long period, they may have difficulty producing clear speech because the constant pressure of the thumb alters the normal positioning of the teeth. This chapter will explore some direct and indirect dental problems that can be caused by prolonged thumb-sucking, and it will explain some of the associated speech problems.

WHAT IS A DENTAL MALOCCLUSION?

When we discuss problems caused by thumb-sucking, we often refer to a condition known as a *dental malocclusion.*

In order to understand what a dental malocclusion is, it is helpful to understand the structure of the oral cavity, or mouth. The dental arches are the bony structures of the mouth that support the teeth. There are two dental arches—the upper arch, or *maxilla,* which is part of the skull; and the lower arch, which is called the *mandible,* or jaw. Dental malocclusions are described as crooked or incorrectly positioned teeth, an improper bite relationship between the teeth in the upper and lower arches, or a malformation of the bone of the dental arches. A dental malocclusion can involve one or a combination of these conditions.

HOW DOES PROLONGED SUCKING CAUSE MALOCCLUSION?

Dental literature has abundant research that describes the harmful effects of prolonged sucking habits on dental growth and development. Just as the controlled pressure of orthodontic appliances can move teeth, the pressure applied by a thumb, finger, or pacifier can influence the position of the teeth and the formation of the bony structures of the mouth. The degree of malformation depends on the direction of these forces and on the duration, frequency, and intensity of the sucking activity. A study by the United States Public Health Service, Division of Health Statistics, concluded that thumb-sucking can cause severe cases of *open-bite* and *overjet*—problems that will be discussed later in this chapter. In my own practice, 94 percent of my thumb-sucking patients have suffered some type of dental malocclusion resulting from their sucking habits. Although no broad studies have tried to link thumb-sucking with the need for orthodontic care, it is probable that a large percentage of an orthodontist's caseload is the result of patients' sucking habits. A study of 15,000 children in one orthodontic clinic concluded that 60 percent of the dental malocclusions found in these patients were caused by their sucking habits.

The Normal Bite

In order to recognize the different types of dental problems related to thumb-sucking and how they may influence oral muscle function, it is a good idea to understand what a normal bite is. In a normal bite relationship, the upper teeth fit over the lower teeth like a lid on a box. (See Figure 3.1.) When a person with a normal bite chews or bites down, the pressure is evenly distributed throughout the mouth. In this way, no one area is over-stressed.

Anterior Dental Malocclusions

The malocclusions we will discuss in this section involve

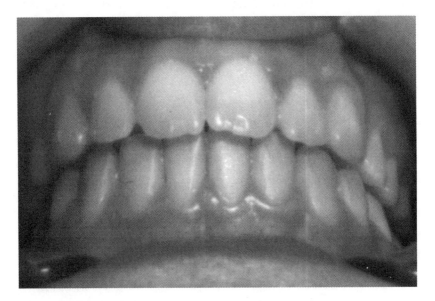

Figure 3.1. Normal Bite

problems in the front, or *anterior,* of the mouth. As you read the following descriptions, refer to Figure 3.1, which shows a normal bite. This will enable you to compare differences between a normal bite relationship and an abnormal bite relationship that has been caused by prolonged thumb-sucking.

The Anterior Open-Bite

The most common type of dental malocclusion associated with sucking habits is the *anterior open-bite.* My data on 723 patients reveal that an incredible 88 percent had varying degrees of this disorder. People with an anterior open-bite cannot bring their lower and upper front teeth together when they bring their back teeth together. (See Figure 3.2.) Therefore, the pressures of biting and chewing are absorbed by the teeth that are able to come together. For those who suffer from anterior open-bite, the unevenly distributed pressure during chewing may cause them to clench and grind their teeth. The cusps of those teeth absorbing the pressure may break off. Other problems may develop such

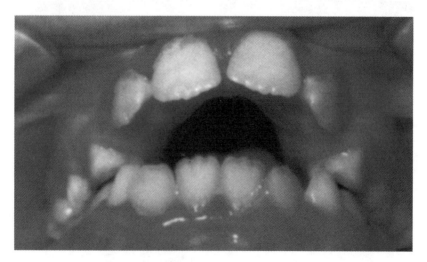

Figure 3.2. Anterior Open-Bite

as oral muscle fatigue, spasms, and problems of the *temporomandibular joint*, or TMJ disorder. Individuals with an anterior open-bite have difficulty chewing efficiently, and avoid eating foods such as corn on the cob and apples because they are not able to bring the upper and lower teeth together to bite into these foods.

Tongue Thrust

Tongue thrust, which is present in 97 percent of people with a front open-bite, is sometimes called *infantile swallow.* This is because all babies swallow in this manner, with the tongue functioning low and forward in the mouth.

A mature swallow evolves with normal growth and development, with the tongue moving upward to create a seal between the tongue and the roof of the mouth, or *palate.* However, an anterior open-bite forces a continuation of the forward thrusting pattern because the tongue has to seal off the gap between the upper and lower front teeth. Children with this type of swallowing disorder often complain of stomach discomfort, which may be due to excessive swallowing of air. Over time, the open-bite may become more severe as the teeth are continually pushed forward by a combination of the tongue thrust and the thumb-sucking activity.

If an individual with tongue thrust has orthodontic treatment to correct the dental malocclusion, the tongue function usually improves or adapts to the new corrected dental environment. But if the tongue thrust continues, the ongoing pressure of the tongue against the teeth can undermine the stability the orthodontic correction.

Overjet and/or Maxillary Protrusion

The pressure of the thumb against the upper front teeth or bone can cause the teeth or the entire upper front bony structure to develop forward, creating an *overjet* and/or *maxillary protrusion.* Children who have protruding front teeth experience *twice* the dental trauma and fracture to these teeth than children who do not have an overjet.

If the protrusion of the upper front teeth is significant, it becomes difficult to bring the lips together. People with this problem tend to have their mouths open most of the time. And since the mouth doesn't have a filtering mechanism, as the nose does, air-borne bacteria and viruses have unrestricted access through the habitually open mouth. Furthermore, these individuals often have difficulty collecting saliva efficiently. Instead of remaining in the mouth, the saliva tends to pool in the corners of the mouth, and excessive drooling may be a problem.

Class II Jaw Relationship

In a *class II jaw relationship,* the lower jaw and teeth are too far back behind the upper dental arch. Although this condition is thought to be hereditary, there is no doubt that pressure applied by the thumb to the upper front teeth contributes to its development. According to my data, 34 percent of my thumb-sucking patients have a class II jaw relationship.

Posterior Dental Malocclusions

Posterior dental malocclusions are problems affecting the teeth, dental arches, and palate at the back of the oral cavity. Whereas many anterior malocclusions are caused by the continual pressure of the thumb, posterior problems are often caused by the pressure of the muscles in the cheeks and tongue. During sucking activity, the muscles in the cheeks contract inward against the upper dental arch, which contributes to its narrowing. At the same time, the sides of the tongue move outward in a sideways, or lateral, direction against the lower arch, which promotes the expansion of the lower dental arch. Thus, one or more of the upper side or back teeth may become positioned *inside*, rather than outside, the lower dental arch. Figure 3.3 shows how the oral-facial muscles function while the child is sucking.

Posterior Cross-Bite

Numerous studies have demonstrated that thumb-sucking and pacifier-sucking habits contribute to the development of a *posterior cross-bite*. A study in Sweden determined that 20 percent of 445 pacifier-sucking children had a posterior cross-bite; and my data reveal that 25 percent of my thumb-sucking patients have had some degree of cross-bite. There are two types of posterior cross-bite—*bilateral*, or two-sided, cross-bite; and *unilateral*, or one-sided, cross-bite.

Bilateral Cross-Bite. *Bilateral cross-bite* is a condition in which a number of the upper teeth on *both* sides of the mouth are in cross-bite. In severe cases of bilateral cross-bite, such as the one represented in Figure 3.4, the upper dental arch can become fixed within the lower arch, which

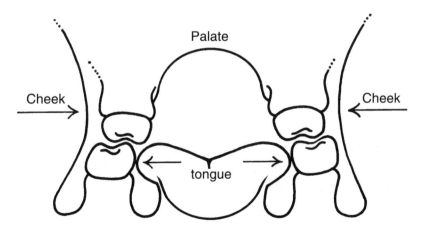

Figure 3.3. Oral-Facial Muscles During Sucking Activity

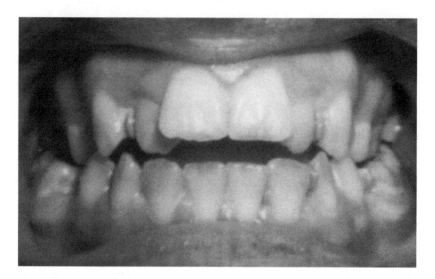

Figure 3.4 Bilateral Cross-Bite With Crowded Teeth

means that the upper arch will not grow properly in width. Instead, it becomes high and narrow. A narrow upper dental arch promotes crowding of all the teeth in this arch. In addition, when the palate is high and narrow, the tongue is not able to make an efficient seal with the palate in order to execute a proper swallow. Thus, the problem of tongue thrust and its associated speech problems may develop.

Unilateral Cross-Bite. The most common type of posterior cross-bite is a *unilateral—one-sided—cross-bite*. One of the most destructive results of this type of posterior cross-bite is that it can cause the lower jaw to shift to the side during biting and chewing. Figure 3.5 illustrates the problem of unilateral cross-bite with mandibular shift, or shifting of the jaw. This lateral shifting causes or contributes to several significant problems:

• *Lateral /s/ lisp.* The lateral lisp is a speech impediment, which we will discuss later in the chapter.

- *Bruxing or grinding of the teeth.* This results from the efforts of the upper and lower teeth to maintain a functional relationship when the patient bites down. Tooth mobility and gum recession may result from grinding.

- *Accidental laceration or chewing of the inner cheeks.* The cheeks often get in the way when the lower arch has to shift laterally for biting and chewing.

- *TMJ disorder (temporomandibular joint disorder).* The temporomandibular joint connects the lower jaw to the skull and is a ball-and-socket hinge mechanism that controls the functional relationship of the upper and lower teeth and dental arches. This hinge is the mechanism that allows the mouth to open and close. The unilateral crossbite is a significant cause of TMJ disorder. Some problems associated with TMJ disorder are pain in the head, face, ear, neck and shoulder; osteoarthritis; limited ability to open the mouth; muscle spasm; dislocation and locking of the jaw; vertigo, and ringing ear noise. Treatment of temporomandibular joint problems can be extremely complex.

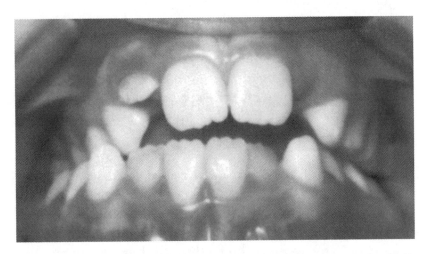

Figure 3.5. Complete Unilateral Cross-Bite With Mandibular Shift

Lingual Tipping

Another type of dental malocclusion can occur when the child habitually positions the thumb against the outside of the lower front teeth. In this case, the inward pressure of the thumb against these teeth can cause them to tip *inward* toward the tongue.

Eruption of Teeth in Thumb-Sucking Individuals

We have learned about the problems involved in the formation of the dental structures that can result from prolonged and constant thumb-sucking. But why do changes in the shape of the mouth create such problems with the teeth? This is because the upper and lower teeth will always try to make contact with one another. In fact, teeth will continue to *erupt*, or grow, until they make contact with a tooth on the opposite dental arch. For this reason, it is important to replace a lost permanent tooth with a bridge. If it is not replaced, the tooth in the opposite arch will begin to over-erupt in an effort to make contact with the missing tooth. Figure 3.6 illustrates the problem.

When there is an anterior over-bite due to a thumb-sucking habit, the upper and lower front teeth may over-erupt in an effort to make contact with one another. This overeruption disturbs the functional relationship between the dental arches because the crowns of the overerupting teeth become higher than those of the teeth surrounding them.

Root Resorption in Primary and Permanent Teeth

In normal development, the pressure of the permanent teeth pushing up under the primary teeth causes *root resorption*. This loosens the teeth until they become mobile

Over-Erupted Tooth

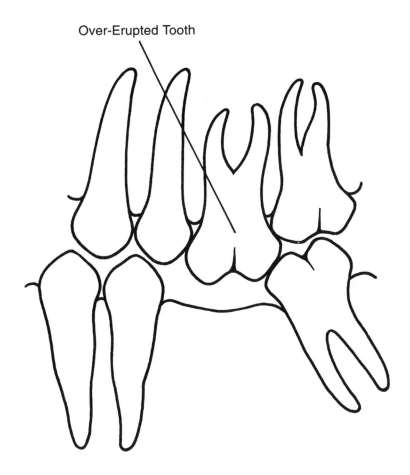

Figure 3.6. Over-Erupted Tooth

and fall out. This normal process, which begins around age six, prepares for the eruption of the permanent teeth.

But when thumb-sucking is excessive, the constant pressure can cause resorption earlier than normal, and the baby tooth may be lost prematurely—before the permanent tooth is *ready* to erupt. This can lead to several problems. First, the bone can reform over the top of the space left by the baby tooth, slowing the eruption of the permanent tooth and making it more difficult. Second, the adjacent teeth may drift into the gap created by the lost baby tooth. Then, when the permanent tooth is ready to come in, the space is already filled, resulting in crowding of the teeth. In addition, if the sucking habit continues after the eruption of the permanent upper front teeth—the incisors—the roots of these teeth may experience resorption.

It is important to note that teeth that have suffered resorption are twice as likely to experience further resorption with orthodontic treatment. It is therefore clear that it is important to try to eliminate thumb-sucking habits prior to the eruption of the permanent upper incisors—an event that occurs between ages six and eight. If the thumb-sucking habit is not eliminated, these teeth, like baby teeth, could become mobile and eventually be lost. And, of course, there are no replacements for permanent teeth.

HOW DOES THUMB-SUCKING AFFECT SPEECH?

We now know that sucking habits can cause many dental problems, and they can influence the swallowing pattern; and, as we saw in the last chapter, these habits can cause significant emotional and psychological pain. Furthermore, prolonged thumb-sucking may cause or exacerbate speech impediments because it changes the normal shape of the mouth—the instrument that produces sound and speech.

Lisping

Lisping is a common problem in many children. One form of lisping is called /s/ speech distortion—that is, the inability to produce a clear /s/ sound. A five-year study of lisping in 371 thumb-sucking children between the ages of six and nine years found that 26 percent were active thumb-suckers. The study determined that thumb-suckers make significantly more errors for /s/ and /z/ sounds than non-thumb-sucking children. In my own study of thumb-sucking children, 38 percent exhibited a lisping problem.

The anterior open-bite can aggravate a lisping problem because the tongue can easily slide through the gap between the upper and lower front teeth. This results in a /th/ sound—for instance, *thithter* instead of *sister*. The /t/, /d/, /L/, and /n/ sounds may also be formed *between* the teeth instead of behind the upper front teeth.

Tongue thrust can interfere with correct pronunciation of certain sounds, requiring that the tongue move up and back in the mouth. These sounds may include /s/, /z/, /sh/, /ch/, /j/, /r/, /t/, /d/, /L/, and /n/.

In cases of a unilateral posterior cross-bite, the lateral shift of the lower jaw can intensify or contribute to the development of a lateral /s/ lisp—a slushy sounding /s/—because the tongue and air escape from the side of the mouth as the jaw shifts.

The prognosis for successful correction of a lisp is not good if the thumb-sucking habit continues along with a tongue thrust. Many patients who experience one or both of these problems undergo years of speech therapy with little or no results. It is a frustrating experience for both therapist and child.

Other Speech Impediments

Protruding upper front teeth create pronunciation problems for /f/ and /v/ because in English, these sounds require that the lower lip make contact with the upper front teeth. If the front teeth protrude too much, these sounds are difficult to pronounce properly. The protrusion may also present problems for sounds requiring that the two lips come together, such as /p/, /b/, and /m/.

Parents should be aware that the elimination of sucking habits often results in the improvement of dental and speech problems. This is particularly true when treatment to eliminate a sucking habit is begun *early*. However, if thumb-sucking continues for too long a period, the problems can become more profound.

CONCLUSION—WHAT IS THE POTENTIAL FOR IMPROVEMENT?

Many types of dental malocclusion associated with thumb-sucking habits improve or self-correct if the habit is terminated early. Figures 3.7 through 3.12 are before and after photographs of the mouths of thumb-sucking children who have given up their thumb-sucking habits. These children received no orthodontic treatment. What made their teeth self-correct? When the pressure of constant thumb-sucking was removed, the teeth spontaneously returned to their normal or near-normal state.

We are not claiming that the elimination of a sucking habit is the *only* answer for all individuals. The posterior cross-bite malocclusion, for example, is rarely transitional or self-correcting with the termination of sucking. It is a condition that almost always requires orthodontic treatment. In many cases, once the dental malocclusion has been corrected, the child's speech improves. But when the speech impediment is severe and a tongue-thrusting problem is evident, the child may have to undergo oral myofunctional therapy to correct the tongue thrust, in addition to speech therapy.

We have seen some typical examples of dental, physical, and speech problems that can result from prolonged thumb-sucking. And we have seen that no part of the body functions by itself. Every part of the body has a functional relationship with another part; and the entire body has a

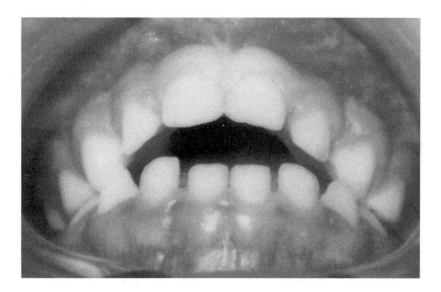

Figure 3.7. Five-Year-Old Before Treatment

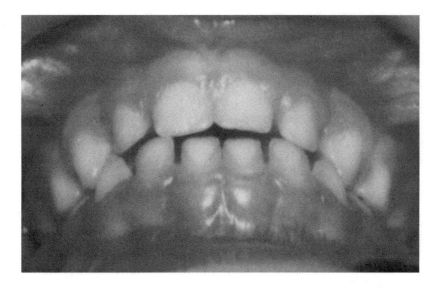

Figure 3.8. Five-Year-Old After Treatment

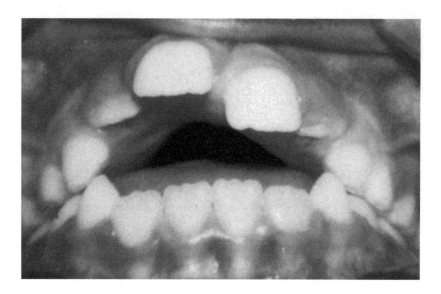

Figure 3.9. Seven-Year-Old Before Treatment

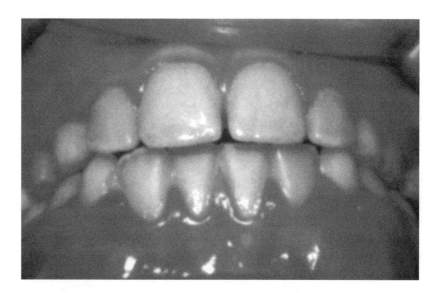

Figure 3.10. Seven-Year-Old After Treatment

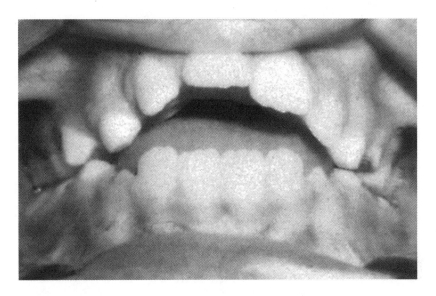

Figure 3.11. Nine-Year-Old Before Treatment

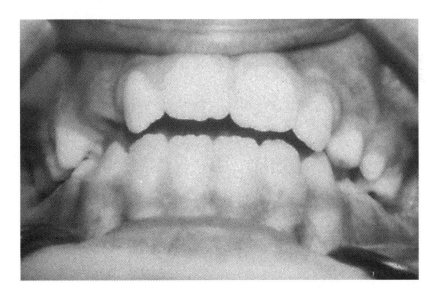

Figure 3.12. Nine-Year-Old After Treatment

relationship with the individual's self-image, ability to function in society, to speak, and to communicate. The important thing is to understand why the problems of prolonged sucking occur, how they affect a person's dental growth and self-image, and, finally, what to do to correct them. Bear in mind that most of the problems discussed in this chapter can be reversed or corrected. If your baby or toddler is sucking, you can assume that the youngster will eventually give up thumb-sucking without your interference. But the behavior should *not* be ignored indefinitely. Although many of the dental and speech problems that result from prolonged sucking habits can be corrected, it makes no sense to allow problems to further develop before initiating treatment. Little mouths deserve a chance to develop normally.

Chapter 4

Other Habits Associated With Prolonged Thumb-Sucking

By now you have learned that thumb-sucking is a complicated activity that can cause deep psychological, emotional, and physical problems. It can affect children's self-esteem, their school work, their social relationships, their dental development, and their ability to speak clearly. In addition, many children develop certain behavior patterns during the sucking activity, which eventually become part of the sucking ritual. These secondary habits are usually discontinued when the thumb-sucking habit is eliminated.

SECONDARY HABITS

In Chapter 2, we spoke about certain habits that children can pick up when they are trying to control their sucking habit in public settings such as school. In this chapter, we will talk about some habits that children may acquire *in addition* to their sucking habit, which sometimes become part of their thumb-sucking ritual. Although some of these habits are not destructive in and of themselves, when they are done to excess, they can lead to other problems.

Hair Twirling

Children with thumb-sucking habits often twirl their hair while they are sucking. Although this may not seem to be a serious problem, it can lead to considerable hair loss. In fact, children with this habit can make themselves almost entirely bald on one side of the head. Some parents try to discourage hair twirling by braiding or cutting the hair, but this usually doesn't stop the behavior. Other parents make their children wear hats; or they punish them in more obvious ways by scolding them or sending them to their room. In most cases, the hair-twirling behavior will stop once the thumb-sucking habit is eliminated. And parents can be reassured that if their child has lost his hair because of excessive hair twirling, it will probably grow back within a short period of time.

Genital Fondling

It is not unusual for children to have one hand in their pants fondling their genitals while thumb-sucking. Genital exploration and fondling is a very common and normal behavior in infants and preschoolers and should not be considered a problem as such. But when it is done in combination with thumb-sucking—that is, when it becomes part of the sucking ritual—it is not likely to go away unless the sucking habit is addressed.

Parents and siblings may be terribly embarrassed by children who fondle themselves in public, and their responses may be harsh. But reprimands and criticism are not helpful. On the contrary, such reactions only make the situation worse. It is important for parents to realize that thumb-sucking children who have picked up a secondary habit will usually give it up once the thumb-sucking activity is eliminated.

Caressing and Ear Rubbing

Many children rub or caress a blanket or other object while sucking. Some children even caress *another person* while sucking their thumb! I had one young patient who sucked her thumb at school, and she had an associated habit that involved rubbing the ear of anyone who happened to be near her while she was sucking. Once her thumb-sucking problem was conquered, the ear-rubbing habit also stopped.

Bedwetting

Some children who have thumbs-sucking habits also have bedwetting problems. Although this problem is not always accompanied by thumb-sucking behavior, there may be a physical explanation for the connection. Many children with a sucking habit suck in order to relax and fall asleep. When they enter the REM stage of sleep—the deepest stage of sleep—the thumb-sucking activity is generally passive. Throughout the night, there are alternating lighter and deeper stages of sleep. During the lighter periods of sleep, the sucking activity resumes, which lulls the child back into deep REM sleep. Thus, the stimulus to wake up and go to the bathroom is possibly inhibited.

Of course, bedwetting alone is not a threat to a child's physical health. But it can be emotionally upsetting and embarrassing for a child. It is a wise parent who seeks help for the child's thumb-sucking habit because it may be contributing to the bedwetting problem.

GENERAL HEALTH PROBLEMS

There are many health problems caused by thumb-sucking habits. In fact, parents often notice that their child's general health has improved once the thumb-sucking habit is discontinued. This is because bacteria no longer have constant access to the child's mouth. But as long as the habit is ongoing—and particularly when there is an ancillary habit that involves nose-picking, touching the genitals, hair, or other people—parents must make sure that children wash their hands on a regular basis.

Impetigo

Impetigo is an inflammatory skin disease characterized by small pustules that become crusted and can rupture. This disease is caused by bacteria—streptococcal or staphylococcal or a combination of both. The rash occurs primarily around the mouth and nostrils. Certain forms of this disease can be highly contagious and particularly problematic for a youngster with a sucking habit because the hands are frequently in close proximity to the rash, which increases the hazard of repeated re-infection or contagion to others.

Pin Worms

Pin worms are small, whitish thin worms that are one-quarter to one-half an inch long. They can infect the large intestine and the anal area, causing considerable itching and irritation. Pin worms are highly contagious. The eggs can be left on a toilet seat by an infected child and picked up by the next person who uses the toilet. A child may get the tiny pin worm eggs on his hands or under the fingernails when scratching the itchy area or wiping after a bowel movement. If the hands are not washed frequently and thoroughly, the eggs can transfer to anything and anyone the child touches. The infection is extremely difficult to eliminate in thumb-sucking children because they are constantly putting their thumb in their mouth.

Crooked Fingers

Only the most extreme cases of thumb-sucking activity cause problems with the formation of the thumb bone. Nevertheless, parents should be aware that intense, frequent sucking of the *fingers* can cause malformations. This is particularly true when the child continues the habit beyond the age of five. Girls have been found to have a higher incidence of crooked fingers due to sucking habits, which is not surprising since more females than males have prolonged habits. In severe cases, the fingers may become rotated or twisted as a result of the sucking activity. Writing skills may be adversely affected because the child has difficulty holding a pencil properly. When sucking habits are terminated, these malformations often improve spontaneously. However, in some cases of severe rotation and hyperextension, surgery may be required to correct the deformity.

Warts and Other Problems

Warts commonly occur on the hands, but they can occur anywhere on the body. They are caused by a virus and result in a rough-surfaced, raised growth on the skin. Warts can spread to the lips or face if a child sucks a thumb or finger infected with warts.

Intense, frequent sucking activity may also cause the thumbnail or fingernail to become extremely sore, and the nail may separate from the skin and become infected.

And, finally, thumb-sucking activity can cause calluses

to develop on the favorite thumb. These can become quite sore, but they generally disappear along with the thumb-sucking habit.

CONCLUSION

At this point, you have learned a great deal about the causes of prolonged thumb-sucking and many of the psychological and physical problems that this behavior can provoke. Our aim here is to inform, not to frighten. Research has demonstrated that the thumb-sucking activity can cause a number of problems. But it is comforting to know that many of these health problems may improve or disappear once the thumb-sucking behavior has been eliminated.

Chapter 5

THE PREVENTION OF PROLONGED SUCKING HABITS

Thumb-sucking in infants is a normal activity as well as a wonderful built-in stress reliever. If your child is under the age of five, her sucking should not be a major cause for concern. Unfortunately, some parents begin working on the elimination of sucking activity in their child before the youngster is able to understand why thumb-sucking is a problem or comprehend the idea of self-control. Remember that your child's thought processes and perceptions of the world around her are quite different from those of an adult, and they will change over time as she grows and develops.

YOUR CHILD'S EMOTIONAL DEVELOPMENT

If thumb-sucking is normal in infants, how can parents prevent it from becoming a prolonged habit? The first step is to understand your child's emotional development and what she needs in order to be healthy and happy. Meeting those needs is the second step.

Your Infant's Needs

According to psychologist Eric Erikson, during the first year of life, infants learn to trust or not to trust the world around them by the way their caretakers respond to them. Happy, well-tended babies cry less and sleep more because they have learned to trust that they will be well cared for. Babies learn this lesson during the first stage of their emotional development.

Crying in infants is *always* a spontaneous response to some sort of discomfort or some physical or emotional need. They haven't planned it; they aren't trying to manipulate their parents by crying. Babies who are pampered and loved feel a sense of well-being and happiness, but they don't connect that happiness with the fact that their parents respond to them when they cry. This is because they have no self-identity—they are not aware that they exist as separate individuals.

Some parents believe that if they respond to every cry of distress, they will spoil the baby; but this is absolutely not true. In fact, it can be harmful if parents do not respond to a crying baby. For example, some parents try to impose a feeding schedule on their infant, and they refuse to respond to her cries when she becomes hungry at the "wrong" time. And when they finally decide the time is right for a feeding, the baby is too distressed to take in nourishment. The feeding takes much longer because the infant has swallowed so much air while crying that frequent burping is necessary. The exhausted infant drifts off to sleep before her hunger is satisfied. Consequently, she wakes up within a short period of time in need of another feeding. The parents experience more tension and more fatigue. And instead of establishing a regular feeding schedule for the infant, they have begun to create an extremely erratic schedule. The only thing the infant learns from this type of treatment is that she cannot trust that her needs will be met. This makes babies anxious, fearful, and much more likely to cry.

The Infant's Thumb-Sucking Activity

As we know, thumb-sucking is normal in infants, and occasional sucking does not indicate that parents are negligent. The problems arise when babies suffer from *regular* periods of boredom, fatigue, hunger, discomfort, or physical and emotional stress. If an infant's needs are taken care of on a regular basis, and if she can count on a meaningful and loving interaction with the people around her, there is much less likelihood that a thumb-sucking habit will be firmly established. It is not an easy task being the parent of an infant. Just remember that by responding when the baby cries, by seeing to her needs, by hugging and singing and talking to her—even when you are absolutely exhausted—you will save time, work, and many problems in the hours, days, and months to come.

Your Toddler's Needs

As your baby grows beyond the infant stage, her needs change, her intellectual capacity increases dramatically, and her sense of self begins to develop. This is the time when parents must learn to recognize the fine line between being a loving, nurturing parent and being an overindulgent parent. All children like to know that they have limits. In fact, if parents cater to their youngster's every whim, the child never learns to tolerate frustration or disappointment, and she will not learn anything about the rights of other people. Overindulged youngsters often have a hard time adjusting to any form of structure or discipline, which means that they may have problems in social relationships and in school or daycare. This can result in isolation and sadness, which, as we know, increases thumb-sucking

behavior. Children such as these have an especially difficult time overcoming their sucking habits because they
have never had to practice any form of self-discipline.

A Structured Day

All children need some form of structure in their day. Days
spent in front of the television set can only encourage
thumb-sucking. It is common for children to begin thumb-
sucking the moment the television is turned on, and obviously children who spend a great deal of time in front of the
television tend to indulge in excessive sucking. It is much
better for children to be busy with other activities, playing
games, running outside, or even helping mom or dad with
simple chores. But if parents occasionally use the television
set as a mechanical babysitter, it can be extremely helpful to
place a small table with toys, crafts, or art materials in front
of the child so that her hands are occupied.

A Safe Haven

Any form of emotional or physical stress will stimulate the
sucking activity. It may be the result of a skinned knee, an
argument with a playmate, or a fast-paced lifestyle. Many
of us have more stress in our lives than our ancestors did.
Consequently, I suspect that there are far more youngsters
in today's society who have prolonged sucking habits. Life
is hectic with both parents in most families working outside the home. And then there are the household chores;
children's sports activities, dancing, gymnastic, and music
lessons; school functions; and a score of additional extra-
curricular activities. The burden of so many commitments
often leaves parents feeling frazzled. Over-scheduling is a
sure path to tension and frustration for the entire family.

If you feel you are under continual pressure, you can be
certain your children feel it too, and they can be over-
whelmed by it. Youngsters need time to be children, to play,

and to spend relaxed one-on-one, quality time with their parents. From time to time, it is necessary to step back and examine commitments. If a heavy schedule of enrichment programs and other activities is promoting stress and preventing adequate time for a positive, meaningful family relationship, it is time to reevaluate your lifestyle. Finding a good balance between work and family is a challenge, but it is possible if parents really evaluate what is important and what is not. Setting priorities and firm limits helps reduce pressure and nurture the family alliance.

Many parents push their children to succeed at any cost. In fact, some youngsters are under so much pressure to excel in everything they do that they eventually resist trying anything new because of fear of failure. Evaluate realistically and appreciate your child's individual capabilities. Parents should give their children praise for all their efforts, even if they don't get the highest scores on their spelling test or get a home run at the baseball game. Naturally, parents cannot provide a stress-free environment for their children, because life is never without some form of stress. But parents can make their children feel that they are in a safe environment where they are accepted and loved for who they are no matter what talents they do or don't have.

Excellent Childcare

Millions of children attend childcare centers, and it can be difficult to control the sucking activity under these circumstances. When considering a childcare facility, ask questions of other parents and make it a point to visit unannounced during working hours. Do the children appear to be happy and busy with a wide choice of activities? Busy children don't have time for excessive thumbsucking. Is there an adequate ratio of staff to children—one adult for every three or four children? If not, you may question whether the staff will have time to offer your child creative play and learning. Inquire about staff turn-over. If it is high, your child will have a difficult time having the intimate, comforting relationship with an adult that is so necessary to her emotional well-being and so instrumental in relieving anxiety that can result from being separated from you.

YOUR CHILD'S INTELLECTUAL DEVELOPMENT

If your child has already established a thumb-sucking habit and you want to avoid entrenching the behavior further, you will find it helpful to learn a little about the early stages of children's intellectual, or cognitive, development. Why? Before the thumb-sucking habit can be eliminated, a child must be old enough to participate and cooperate in a program of elimination. This means that she must be able to understand the problem of prolonged thumb-sucking. According to psychologist Jean Piaget, children develop intellectually in predictable stages that begin at birth and continue until adulthood.

How Infants Learn

No one is born with the ability to reason. It is a faculty that is developed throughout infancy and childhood. Infants learn by touching, feeling, smelling, seeing, and hearing. They explore with their mouths, hands, eyes, and other senses. These sensory experiences play a crucial role in the development of personality, language skills, and intelligence. Parents who continually pull their baby's hand from her mouth or cover her hands to prevent thumb-sucking are doing a terrible injustice—they are interrupting an essential part of their child's development. If you are concerned about your infant's thumb-sucking, keep her busy with lots of activities, talk to her, and give her beautiful things to play with and look at. You'll find that there will be far less time for sucking behavior when all the senses are stimulated.

How Toddlers See the World

Toddlers don't think the same way that older children, adolescents, or adults think. They have a different reality. For example, toddlers have a difficult time understanding the concepts of past and future. If you promise a toddler that you'll give her a treat in a week if she doesn't suck her thumb, you might as well be talking about a hundred years in the future. Your promise may motivate her to begin a program of elimination, but she will forget the reason for stopping the habit from one moment to the next—she will remember only the surprise.

In addition, preschool children usually don't understand the difference between right and wrong. If they are given a prize for not thumb-sucking, they will probably begin sucking again as soon as they have the prize. It's not that they plan to do it; they are not yet able to understand the concept of dishonesty. These children are dominated by sensory impressions: that is, they can only understand that a prize is something good—and so is thumb-sucking!

Although parents may be worried that their toddler's thumb-sucking habit will continue beyond the preschool years, they must remember that it is not appropriate to impose the task of elimination on a child who is not capable of doing anything about it. Setting goals or tasks that a child cannot understand or accomplish can lead to a lasting sense of self-doubt and shame.

The Magic Age of Five

We know from Piaget's work that children cannot and

should not be forced to perform at a level beyond their developmental schedule. Children must be allowed to develop at their own pace. The ideal time for parents to intervene in a thumb-sucking habit is when their child is five years of age. The average five-year-old is intellectually capable of understanding some cause-and-effect relationships: *If I thumb-suck, my teeth will stick out.* They are beginning to realize that other people have a point of view that is different from theirs: *Mom thinks thumb-sucking is bad for children's mouths.* And they can grasp the concepts of past and future: *If I don't suck my thumb for a week, I'm going to get a treat.* Children of this age are also capable of some degree of self-control and self-denial. And they are generally eager to please. Certainly, thumb-sucking can be addressed in children over the age of five, but if your child has not yet reached this magic age, don't make an issue of the behavior.

CONCLUSION

When babies' needs are met—when they are pampered, talked to, played with, well fed, and cared for—they are less likely to establish a prolonged sucking habit as they grow older. When toddlers are active, unpressured, and stimulated, it is highly unlikely that they will carry their thumb-sucking beyond the preschool years. Remember that even the happiest, most active infants and toddlers thumb-suck occasionally, and this should never be a concern for parents. Just as important, by trying to eliminate your child's thumb-sucking habit before she has reached a certain point in her intellectual and emotional development, you can actually do more harm and good.

Chapter 6

EVALUATING THE TIMING AND NEED FOR HABIT ELIMINATION

In the last chapter, we spoke about the connection between the age of a child and the youngster's ability to understand the consequences of a thumb-sucking habit. There is a wrong time and a right time to begin a program of elimination. This chapter will explore some indicators that it is not a good time for intervention, and it will discuss the warning signals that the time is right to help your child eliminate his thumb-sucking habit.

WHEN IS THE WRONG TIME TO CONSIDER INTERVENTION?

All people experience stress and anxiety when they are undergoing a change or transitional phase in their lives. Children with thumb-sucking habits will generally increase their sucking activity during these periods, and there is a risk of relapse if a program to eliminate the habit is initiated. Potentially difficult circumstances must be evaluated from the *child's* perspective, taking into account the youngster's stage of development and experience in life. Some examples that require an appropriate period of adjustment before addressing sucking habits are discussed below.

Major Changes in the Family

There is no family that escapes periods of extreme stress. During those times when your family is being pulled by unusual circumstances, allow your thumb-sucking child to indulge in his habit. In fact, intervention will only make matters worse. Although every family is unique, there are some situations that present common, fairly predictable dilemmas for all.

Separation or Divorce

It is difficult for a child of any age to accept the fact that his parents are separating or getting a divorce, no matter what the circumstances. In addition, many children feel that they are to blame for their parents' problems, even though parents may assure them to the contrary. Children love both their parents, and getting used to the idea that they will no longer remain together as a family is traumatic and certainly not an appropriate time to address the sucking behavior. But when a child has had enough time to adjust and be reasonably comfortable with the situation, a consistent effort on the part of both parents will bring success.

The Arrival of a New Sibling

No matter how parents try to make the arrival of a new baby as easy as possible for their other children, there is bound to be some resentment and jealousy. The older child can't help feeling left out, especially during the first few hectic weeks when the demands of the infant occupy much of the parents' time. This is especially true in the case of the first-born sibling.

Sometimes, parents make the mistake of trying to stop

the sucking behavior of an older sibling when a new baby arrives into the family. This is definitely not the time to do this because the child depends on the thumb-sucking activity for comfort during this difficult period of adjustment. It can take six months or even longer for a child to adjust to the arrival of a new sibling.

Moving to a New Home or New School

Moving can be stressful for the entire family. Parents are preoccupied with the details of relocating, and family life can be pretty chaotic while getting settled in a new home. It is even more difficult for children, who will feel anxious about leaving their old friends and starting a new school.

Attending a new daycare center or school, or even entering kindergarten or the first grade can be cause for stress. If a sucking problem cannot be addressed at least three months before the beginning of the school year, do not initiate a program of elimination until the school year is well under way and your child has adjusted to the transition.

A Change in Parents' Schedule or Circumstances

If one or both parents have scheduled a trip, or if one or both have changed jobs that will significantly change their usual routine, it is best to avoid treating a child's sucking habit until everyone has adjusted. This is particularly true if personal circumstances have changed: if there is illness in the family, a death, or even a major social event or vacation—in short, anything that might create stress for you, your family, or your child.

Car Trips and Vacations

Most children who have sucking habits, suck when riding in the car. Sometimes they do it out of boredom; and other times the motion of the car produces a drowsy, mesmerizing sensation that stimulates the sucking activity. You should be aware of this if you and your family are in the habit of taking long car rides for pleasure, for regular visits to relatives, or for vacations. In addition, vacations away from home often produce excitement, erratic schedules, and excessive fatigue—all strong stimulants for sucking activity. It is best to plan well in advance or wait until you have returned from a trip before beginning a program of elimination.

Other Circumstances

There are many situations that can interfere with your child's resolve to get rid of his sucking habit. But if you try to view potential problems from your child's perspective, you can avoid situations that may set him back and leave him feeling frustrated and upset.

Sleep Disorders

As you know, there is a very strong association between the sucking activity and sleep. If you have significant difficulty getting your child to go to bed, or if he suffers from insomnia or often awakens during the night, you must try to resolve these problems before addressing the sucking habit.

It is important to remember that most children go through a period that psychologists call the *fantasy-oriented stage*. This is a normal stage of development when a child's vivid imagination conjures up all kinds of monsters in the night; and it is not realistic to expect him to give up the comfort of his thumb during this scary time. There are resources listed in the back of this book that will help you deal with your child's sleep disorders.

Holiday Excitement

Even though holidays are usually happy events, the excitement and excessive fatigue often associated with these busy occasions can be strong encouragement for the sucking activity. Parents can also be stressed and absorbed with the holiday preparations. So unless your holiday is going to be relaxed and fairly predictable, put the thumb-sucking issue on the back burner until things have settled back to normal.

Others in the Child's Environment With Sucking Habits

When your child has daily contact with other children who have sucking habits, it becomes even more difficult to fight the urge to suck. If your child is in such a setting, try to take him out of it for several days when you begin the program of elimination. The longer he is not in contact with others who have the same habit, the greater the chance that he will not regress.

> Margaret's mom was a single parent who started work at five every morning. She had to get her seven-year-old daughter up very early in the morning and take her to the home of a woman who took care of her before and after school. Of course, this schedule was difficult for Margaret. Sometimes she was extremely cranky by the time she arrived at the woman's home in the morning. It was too early to stay up, so Margaret went to bed and, of course, sucked her thumb in order to get back to sleep. To compound the problem, several older children who were being cared for by the same woman had sucking habits. Margaret was developing a severe dental malocclusion, and the child-care arrangements were preventing her from overcoming her sucking habit.
>
> When her mother brought her to me for treatment, we decided to postpone her program of

elimination until summer vacation, when the child's grandmother would be able to provide full-time care. Our program of positive behavior modification was started at the beginning of summer vacation and, before the end of the summer, Margaret's habit was a thing of the past. The two deciding factors were the absence of other thumb-sucking children and the constant care of a trusted caregiver.

Although we have not discussed all possible negative situations that can arise, you now have the general idea—unusual times are not suitable for eliminating your child's thumb-sucking habit. In addition, unresolved, ongoing problems only present other obstacles to your child's success, and it is sometimes necessary to seek professional help before addressing the sucking habit.

WHEN IS THE RIGHT TIME TO CONSIDER INTERVENTION?

When your child is five years of age or older and has an ongoing thumb-sucking habit, it may be time to help him overcome the habit. In order to do this successfully, the timing must be right and you and your family must be willing to participate.

The Warning Signs

There are certain warning signs that suggest the need to eliminate your child's thumb-sucking behavior. They fall into four general categories: the time and place the activity occurs, associated behaviors and social problems, dental and other health problems, and speech problems related to thumb-sucking. As you read through the following list of questions to ask yourself, try to be objective. These are only suggested guidelines that may help you determine if there is adequate reason to intervene. The guidelines are as follows:

Time and Place of Thumb-Sucking Activity

- Does the sucking activity take place during the day as well as at bedtime?
- Does the sucking activity take place across two or more settings, such as home and school, or in the presence of others outside the immediate family?
- Does your child avoid spending the night with friends because of fear that his sucking activity during sleep will be discovered?
- Has your child's teacher expressed concern about classroom sucking?
- If the sucking activity takes place at school, is it affecting scholastic achievement or relationships with other children in school?

Associated Behaviors and Social Problems

- If the sucking activity does *not* occur in the classroom, are there other problems such as difficulty sitting still; disruptive behavior; or chewing on clothing, pencils, hair, or fingernails?
- Does the child get negative reactions from peers, relatives, parents, siblings, or others in his environment as a result of the sucking activity?
- If there are negative reactions, does the child appear to be isolating himself, excessively withdrawn, anxious, angry, or aggressive?
- Is the sucking behavior affecting your feelings toward your child in a negative way?

- Does your child appear to be listless because of frequent sucking activity?

- Does your child have a conjoined behavior, such as hair twirling, nose picking, or genital fondling, resulting in negative remarks from those in the child's environment?

- Does the child frequently retreat to the sucking behavior to avoid confrontation rather than asserting himself?

Dental and Other Health Problems

- Does there appear to be a dental malocclusion, such as an anterior open-bite, class II jaw relationship, posterior cross-bite, narrow palate, or protruding teeth, that may be related to the sucking habit?

- Does the child engage in bruxism—the unconscious grinding of teeth?

- Does the child complain of clicking or locking of the jaws, headaches, pain in the ear, neck or shoulder, vertigo, or ringing in the ear?

- Does the child have lacerations on the inner cheeks?

- Does the child drool excessively?

- Is there x-ray evidence of root resorption in the primary or permanent upper front teeth?

- Does the child have difficulty biting with his front teeth?

- Does the child complain about frequent stomachaches that can be related to excessive swallowing of air?

- Does the child have calluses, infected fingernails, or crooked fingers as a result of a sucking habit?

- Does the child experience frequent bacterial infections that may be related to habitually open-lip postures or the frequent placement of the thumb or fingers in the mouth?

Speech Problems

- Do you feel your child's verbal communication is limited because his thumb is frequently in his mouth?
- Is the child's speech difficult to understand?
- Does the child exhibit any of the following errors in his speech? /s/, /z/, /sh/, /ch/, /j/, /t/, /d/, /L/, /n/, /p/, /b/, /m/, /f/, /v/, or /r/?
- Does the child avoid speaking because others don't understand him?

If you feel that your child's thumb-sucking habit is directly related to any of the above, do not assume that you must step in immediately to stop the behavior. The importance of these signals must be weighed against other circumstances in his life. Indeed, there are situations during which you should not address the sucking problem no matter what the child's age.

CONCLUSION

When a sucking habit is in danger of becoming prolonged, it is only natural that parents want to intervene to stop their child's behavior before extensive damage is done. You are aware of the warning signs, and you are armed with the knowledge that there are circumstances that make it unrealistic *for the time being* to eliminate your child's thumb-sucking habit. Remember to deal with one problem at a time. This is the best way to insure that your child will conquer the thumb-sucking habit once and for all.

Chapter 7

Taking the First Steps

If you have decided that intervention in your child's thumb-sucking habit is appropriate, there are some important considerations that will help you maximize success and minimize frustration. This information will help you avoid many problems before they occur, and enable you to handle any problems that do occur in a more effective way. You will then be able to assist your child in a confident, sensible, compassionate, and positive way.

WHAT CAN PARENTS DO?

By now, it is clear that early intervention is the best means of preventing the dental, speech, social, and health problems that are associated with a prolonged thumb-sucking habit. You must also remember that, given the complexity of sucking habits, many children become extremely frustrated when they don't experience immediate success. There are, however, things you can do to smooth the way for your child.

Parent Effectiveness Training (PET)

No matter what the situation is, you can help your child by using the following advice of Dr. Thomas Gordon, the creator of PET, or Parent Effectiveness Training, a highly respected program that teaches positive conflict resolution and effective parent-child communication methods. Gordon suggests that parents use "I messages" to let children know how an undesired behavior makes them feel. For example, you might say something to this effect: "I'm concerned about your thumb-sucking. I don't want people to make fun of you because I know it hurts your feelings"; or, "When you feel that you'd like to work on getting rid of the habit, let me know and I'll help you as much as I can. In the meantime, we won't worry about it." Most psychologists agree that this is much more productive than giving your child negative "you messages" such as, "You're acting like a baby when you suck your thumb!" This "you message" criticizes, blames, lowers self-esteem, and provokes rebellion rather than cooperation.

Your child is much more likely to express the desire to stop the sucking activity if the tension over the behavior is alleviated. There is nothing more effective for the relief of tension than giving your child an honest "I message." It lifts the burden from both of you.

Validate Your Child's Feelings

Dr. Gordon also suggests giving positive "you messages" to your child. Remember that when a child tries to give up thumb-sucking, it may be her first encounter with personal hardship. If parents let their child know that they understand how difficult it is to break a thumb-sucking habit, it will help the youngster continue. Acknowledge your child's feelings with positive remarks—"I know how difficult this is for you"—rather than negative ones—"You'll get over it."

One of the great benefits to this approach is that it encourages children and parents to communicate with one another. If there are specific problems that are causing the child to relapse, she will be more likely to communicate those problems if she is sure that you will validate her feelings. The ability to communicate is extremely important to the process of habit elimination. In addition, sympathetic, comforting responses from mom and dad do wonders for soothing emotional setbacks.

Be Consistent

Because young children are not patient, any young child who tries to accomplish a task and experiences problems is likely to to become frustrated. In fact, the child who is trying to stop sucking will perceive *any* lapse as a failure. Therefore, your child will have to experience immediate success if she is to maintain her determination. To accomplish this, you must be consistent, available, and mindful of those situations in which the sucking tends to occur. If you waver in your determination to help your child, or if you allow events or people to interfere with your steadfastness, your child will have a much more difficult time trying to reach her goal. So before you and your child decide to eliminate the thumb-sucking habit, be sure that nothing will hinder or undermine your plans.

During the initial period of habit elimination, make sure that your child follows a regular schedule of meals, activities, and rest periods. Remember that hunger and fatigue produce irritability, and that erratic schedules produce anxiety—all of which stimulate the desire to thumb-suck.

Don't Overindulge Your Child

Parents are often so eager to have their child overcome the

sucking habit that once the child has begun a program of elimination, they become fearful of upsetting her, and they often overlook misbehavior for this reason. If your child threatens to suck because she wants to have her own way or is in need of discipline, be empathetic, but firm. If you don't stand your ground, you will be allowing your child to make *you* responsible for her sucking behavior. Giving in will solve the immediate problem, but the chance of relapse will be great if your child doesn't learn to handle discipline and emotional setbacks without resorting to thumb-sucking. You can act as a parent and still reassure your child that you are her ally and that you are with her in her struggle to discontinue the sucking habit. But it is your child who is ultimately responsible for breaking the habit.

Time It Correctly

Before beginning a program of elimination, allow at least three days of focused, positive support to keep your child busy, occupied, and distracted from the sucking behavior. Weekends are a good time to begin working on the elimination of a sucking habit. They are generally less hectic, and many difficulties associated with the bedtime and naptime sucking activity will be alleviated. The chances for success are even greater if a working parent can take a day of vacation on either Friday or Monday and allow the child to stay home from school or daycare that extra day. School vacations also work well as long as a parent will be available.

Enlist the Help of Siblings

Brothers and sisters can be a tremendous help to your thumb-sucking child. In fact, when you enlist their help, it will make them feel special and proud of the task before them. But you must be careful to explain their role: you don't want police officers or tattlers—you want helpers. Explain how hard it can be to break habits, and how important their help is to both you and the child with the habit. Tell them that this a special problem that can ruin children's teeth and make it difficult to speak properly, and that other children make fun of the sucking activity, which is very hurtful. If you explain the situation honestly and clearly, siblings will understand, and they will be more than willing to cooperate with efforts to eliminate a brother's or sister's thumb-sucking habit.

Encourage siblings to offer praise and encouragement to the youngster trying to discontinue a sucking habit. This support can make an immense difference in bringing about a positive outcome, especially if the declaration of confidence is coming from a favorite older sibling.

Eliminate the "Blankie"

Many children have an attachment to an object such as a blanket, stuffed animal, cloth diaper, pillow, or piece of satin. Their devotion to these transitional objects is a normal part of healthy development. Children hold on to these "blankies" because they are part of the world in which they feel safe and secure, particularly when they are in unfamiliar territory or in need of comfort.

The accessory object may or may not present a problem. Some children become very attached to these items, and it can be difficult for them to give up their thumb and their cherished object at the same time. Other children don't always insist on having their object with them, and their sucking activity is not necessarily connected with it. But for many children, the "blankie" is part of the sucking ritual as well as a stimulus for the activity. In these cases, the best plan of action is to try to eliminate it before tackling the thumb-sucking habit.

> I frequently tell youngsters about the special blanket I had when I was a young child, and how every time I saw or felt my blanket, my thumb wanted to pop right into my mouth! I was so attached to my "blankie" that whenever my mother washed it and hung it out to dry, I would sit under the clothesline and hold on to it as it was drying. One day, when I was about six years of age, mother said, "I know your blanket is very special, but it seems that it makes you want to suck your thumb, and I'm concerned about that old thumb making your smile all crooked. Besides, your blanket is getting pretty worn out. How about if we put it away while it's still in one piece so you can save it for your babies when you grow up?" To soften the blow, she cut off a small piece of the blanket so I could keep it with me. We placed the rest of it in a box, wrapped it with beautiful paper, tied it with a bow, and put it away, out of my sight. I remember that it was hard, but my mother's reverence for my feelings made it a surmountable hurdle, and I stopped my sucking habit once the blanket was gone.

How to Go About It

If you want to eliminate your child's transitional object of affection, you should begin limiting its use for a couple of months before initiating a program to eliminate the thumb-sucking habit. For example, when you're going out together, try leaving the object in the car. If the object is some sort of cloth, you can cut off a small piece for your child to carry in her pocket. After a while, try leaving the object at home.

When your child becomes more comfortable doing without it, you can try to limit its use to a few hours during the day and at bedtime. Then gradually restrict its use to bedtime. When your child has fallen asleep, move the object so that it is not in close proximity, but leave it in the room. The next morning, you might say something to this effect: "Wow! You slept all night without your blanket and I'll bet that old thumb didn't sneak into your mouth nearly as much! How about trying to go to sleep without it? We'll leave it in your room where you can see it, but let's try to go to sleep without it, okay?"

A progress chart can be very helpful during this final stage. Give your child lots of praise and a little reward the first time she has fallen asleep without it. Reward again after one week of falling asleep without it. After two or three weeks without the object, the child will probably be ready to begin addressing the sucking habit.

Some children simply cannot part with their cherished object and are able to stop sucking without giving it up. But if you notice that your child continues to have lapses in the sucking activity because of the presence of her "blankie," it's better to stop the program and wait until she is ready to give it up.

As I mentioned in Chapter 1, my own daughter sucked two fingers and had two cherished "blankies." After having worked with hundreds of children with sucking habits, I knew it was better not to broach the subject of her sucking activity until she was developmentally ready. She was not quite five years of age when she came to me one day without any prompting and said, "Mom, you help all the other children stop sucking their thumbs; why don't you help me?" I was quite surprised and asked her if she was really ready to give it up. She was willing, so we decided to try. However, she was not ready to part with her precious "blankies" and continued having sucking lapses whenever she got her hands on them. I didn't want her to be frustrated or feel bad about herself, so I told her not to worry about it; someday she would be ready to get rid of her habit, and it was okay to wait awhile. But she was determined. She took me into her bedroom and asked me to put her beloved blankets on the highest shelf in her closet so that she couldn't reach them. She knew she wouldn't be able to conquer her habit as long as her "blankies" were accessible. I told her I would lift her up and she could throw the blankets up to the top shelf herself. She put her "blankies" up to her nose to enjoy their scent, and then gently and lovingly pressed them to her cheek for the last time to say good-bye. Then she threw them as hard as she could so that they floated all the way up and landed on the top shelf. For the next two weeks, she would go into her closet and look up at them, but she never asked me to get them down for her. Once the blankets were out of her reach, she was able to discontinue her thumb-sucking habit.

WHAT CAN PARENTS EXPECT?

Even when the situation and timing for elimination of your child's sucking habit are ideal, you can expect that things will not run perfectly. Saying good-bye to this habit produces fairly predictable reactions in most children. If you know what to anticipate, it will make the transition much easier for you and for your child.

Withdrawal Symptoms

The first three to four days without thumb-sucking will be the most difficult and the most critical. You can expect your child to be irritable for a few days while her body chemistry is adjusting to diminished endorphin production and its associated pleasurable sensations. In addition, learning to fall asleep and stay asleep without sucking may add to her irritability. These difficulties subside after several days of consistent abstinence, when the cycle of the habit begins to break down. Around the third or fourth day, the child's body chemistry begins to adjust, and she begins to feel more comfortable without the sucking activity. From this point, each day of sustained, complete abstinence enhances the child's self-confidence, perseverance, and determination. Generally, after the first week of complete withdrawal, the motion of the thumb going to the mouth during the day is minimal or absent.

If There Is a Fingernail-Biting Habit

To my knowledge, I have never had a child substitute another behavior as a result of giving up a sucking habit through my program of positive behavior modification. However, approximately 30 percent of the children I have seen for thumb-sucking habits also have fingernail-biting habits.

If your child is also a nail-biter, your may observe an increase in this behavior while she is trying to discontinue the sucking activity. In addition, most children trying to overcome their sucking habits will frequently have their hands in close proximity to the mouth even though they are not sucking. Parents should avoid making remarks about either of these other behaviors. Commenting about every little thing will surely lead to antagonism and frustration. It is best to work on eliminating one behavior at a time, in order to achieve success overall.

IF YOU NEED OUTSIDE HELP

Some people feel more confident if they have the help of a professional third party. This doesn't mean that this person does all the work while the parents do nothing. On the contrary, parental involvement is still essential for the child's success in eliminating her habit. Nonetheless, a trained professional understands the thumb-sucking behavior and can offer guidance and support that will make the transition as smooth as possible.

Motivational Benefits of Outside Help

Children are often best motivated by the encouragement and suggestions of a caring third party. One reason for this is that parents are too emotionally involved, which makes it difficult for them to be objective. For example, have you ever tried to help your youngster with homework only to find yourself and the child in an emotional gridlock? This can happen even when the parent is a trained teacher.

I once had three patients—all siblings—who had thumb-sucking habits. Their mother was a teacher, educated in child development and trained in behavior modification techniques. Although she had enough academic knowledge to help her children, she knew that an impartial professional would have a stronger influence and would be able to motivate her children far better than she could.

Over the years, I have found that parents are extremely surprised by the effectiveness of third-party intervention. In fact, I have received hundreds of letters from parents who are grateful that they turned to professional guidance.

The Trained Therapist

A professionally trained third party can prevent many problems between parents and their children because the third party makes the rules. In this way, he or she can stop the arguments and tension that commonly occur when parents try to eliminate their child's sucking habit. The therapist enters the child's world as a partner and facilitator, enabling the youngster to feel confident and comfortable. This prompts most children to respond with cooperation, consistency, and minimal frustration. In addition, they have the potential to experience feelings of success from the very first day of therapy. Remember that success builds confidence and perseverance!

The therapist is trained to help children take responsibility for their habit, which in turn motivates them to take responsibility for it. These two steps are imperative before they can let go of the habitual behavior. In order to motivate a child to accept responsibility for eliminating a sucking habit, there must be a strong trust relationship. This is made possible by the participation of a trained, objective individual who will not criticize the child because of her behavior. The child feels a sense of security in knowing the therapist will be tolerant, patient, and empathetic. And she feels safe knowing that she can change her mind without feeling ashamed or guilty.

The Certified Oral Myologist

Certified oral myologists are professionals who are specially trained to help children overcome sucking habits. They belong to the International Association of Orofacial Myology (IAOM), a non-profit organization founded in 1972. The multidisciplinary membership includes speech pathologists, dentists, orthodontists, dental hygienists, and other health professionals. The association is the only international accrediting organization for this therapeutic specialty.

In addition to general academic preparation—including courses in physical, social, and behavioral sciences; oral medicine; orofacial myology; speech pathology; and education—certification requires both specific and comprehensive knowledge and proficiency in the treatment of prolonged thumb-sucking habits through the use of positive behavior modification. Furthermore, certified oral myologists understand cognitive and emotional development and the biological, physiological, and psychological aspects of the thumb-sucking behavior.

Positive behavior modification techniques for the elimination of thumb-sucking are practiced successfully by members of IAOM in the United States as well as Canada, South America, Europe, and Asia. These trained professionals can generally help your child discontinue the sucking habit quickly, without coercion, and in an enjoyable and positive way.

I recommend enlisting the help of a certified oral myologist if:

- You have tried to communicate with your child about making an effort to discontinue the sucking habit, but have not been able to motivate her.
- You have already tried many techniques to eliminate your child's sucking activity without success.
- Gentle reminders have turned into nagging, and the atmosphere in your home has become one of conflict, antagonism, and frustration.
- One parent is not consistent about following through or supporting the necessary procedures.
- There are two or more children in one family with a sucking habit.

To find out if there are any certified oral myologists practicing in your area, contact the International Association of Orofacial Myology at one of the following numbers or sites:

2315 187 Avenue, NE
Redmond, WA 98052-6011
(425) 747–5697
Web Site: http://www.iaom.com
E-Mail: iaomoffice@aol.com

CONCLUSION

It is extremely difficult to give up the comforting sensations of the sucking activity, especially if the habit has been around for a number of years. Children come to depend on climbing into their favorite chair and relaxing with their thumb, especially at the end of a long day. Now they must learn to contend with a number of difficult situations without the comfort of their thumb. The salve that will reduce inner turmoil and lift your child's spirit will be your understanding, patience, and positive support.

Chapter 8

ELIMINATING THE DAYTIME SUCKING HABIT

You now understand the biological, physiological, and psychological aspects of the thumb-sucking behavior. You are aware of the importance of picking an appropriate time to eliminate the habit based on your child's cognitive and emotional development and individual circumstances. You have done your planning and are ready to go for it! Remember that you are the most important person in your child's life. Think positively and expect the best; for if you expect the worst, your expectations are likely to be fulfilled. We will begin by learning what positive behavior modification is and how to apply it. And we will learn some methods to keep everything running on course.

WHAT IS POSITIVE BEHAVIOR MODIFICATION?

Positive behavior modification is a motivational program designed to eliminate an undesirable behavior through positive and negative reinforcement. A series of well-defined goals is established, and after each goal is accomplished a reward is given. The reward reinforces the new, or modified, behavior.

Positive behavior modification for the elimination of a thumb-sucking habit is a three-stage process that involves:

1. Establishing a baseline for the behavior—figuring out when and where the activity occurs.
2. Motivating the child to want to stop the behavior.
3. Positive and negative reinforcement—offering positive reinforcement in the form of praise, encouragement, and rewards to maintain motivation and cooperation; or applying negative reinforcement in the form of withholding rewards until the desired goal is accomplished.

HOW SHOULD YOU PROCEED?

You will take one step at a time and proceed at a pace that is comfortable for you and your child. And you can feel confident that, having read this book up to this point, you are well prepared for the task ahead.

Establish a Baseline

The first step is to establish a baseline for the sucking behavior. Simply put, how frequently and under what circumstances does the sucking occur? For example, does your child thumb-suck at school, at the movies, when he is irritated or fatigued, when he is riding in a car, or engaged in another activity such as reading? Kindergartners and first-graders frequently suck during story-time, quiet-time, a film, or toward the end of the school day when they are tired. For this reason, it is a good idea to check with your child's teacher or daycare provider to find out when your youngster tends to resort to sucking behavior. Be sure to write this information down as a reminder in the days ahead. Once you have established when and under what circumstances your child is thumb-sucking, you will be able to proceed to the next step.

Motivate Your Child to Stop

If your child is not motivated to stop sucking his thumb, he won't cooperate. But there are many things you can do to motivate him. Begin by educating your youngster just as you have educated yourself. Be honest about your concerns, and don't underestimate his ability to understand what you are talking about.

While I am working on the motivational phase of habit elimination, I tell my young patients that smiles are very special because they are the nicest thing one person can give to another. I also use photographs and models of teeth to help children see the difference between normal teeth and teeth that are out of alignment because of a sucking habit.

I often ask the child if he knows what braces are and how they work. Children can generally grasp the idea that braces apply pressure to the teeth. I explain that some children have crooked teeth, so they get braces on their teeth to make them nice and straight. And I explain exactly how the braces straighten teeth.

You have certainly learned enough at this point to do the same with your child. Keep the explanation simple: braces straighten teeth by pushing on them until they are moved into just the right position so each tooth on top fits together with the tooth below it. When all the teeth fit together properly, the upper teeth can work with the bottom teeth to chew food and to make a beautiful, healthy-looking smile. Using this explanation as a guide, you can explain how the thumb also has the power to move teeth, but in the wrong direction!

If your child's teeth are crooked, you can use a mirror to show him just what is happening to his own teeth. Your dentist may also have models of teeth that will help him understand the process.

If you speak to your child with respect, and tell him about some of the things you have learned in this book, he will respond. Your patience, knowledge, and willingness to encourage your child are the strongest motivational tools at your disposal.

Warning: Don't Make Bargains

If you are tempted to motivate your child by promising to change your own behavior, don't do it. For example, don't promise your child that you will quit smoking or lose ten pounds or run a marathon if he stops thumb-sucking! This type of negotiating puts the responsibility for the child's habit on *you*. In addition, if you are not able to live up to your part of the bargain, your child will have an excellent reason not to give up the thumb-sucking behavior.

Begin Positive Reinforcement

Everything you have done up to this point has been preparation for the main event—elimination of the thumb-sucking behavior. It will be necessary for your child to stay on task long enough to ensure that the habit is completely extinguished. This usually takes three months. There are four things you can do to make the transition smooth and even enjoyable. They involve creating progress charts, drawing up a contract with your child, setting definite goals, and providing positive reinforcement.

Create Progress Charts

A progress chart is an excellent way to keep track of your child's progress. Allow him to participate and make this a memorable and enjoyable project for both of you! In addition, charts give children a visual sense of time, and they are a source of immediate gratification. These are essential for continued motivation to stay on task.

Make a trip to the store to buy some brightly colored poster board, markers, crayons, and stickers. You and your child will create two charts—a two-day, or forty-eight-hour, chart and a three-month chart.

The two-day chart will help make the task seem less overwhelming for your youngster. Separate the days into three time slots—morning, afternoon, and bedtime—using Figure 8.1 as a guide. When you have finished, hang the chart in a place that can be reached by your child. If your child does

I'm Going To Kick My Thumb Habit Away!		
Morning	Afternoon	Bedtime
HOORAY! I DIDN'T SUCK FOR ONE WHOLE DAY!		
Morning	Afternoon	Bedtime
HOORAY! I'M ON MY WAY. I DIDN'T SUCK FOR TWO WHOLE DAYS!		

Figure 8.1. Two-Day Progress Chart

not suck all morning, allow him to place a sticker in the morning time slot. Repeat for the successful completion of the afternoon and bedtime periods. After the successful completion of two consecutive days without sucking, the child is ready for a three-month chart.

The three-month chart can be divided by placing six weeks on the front of the chart and six weeks on the back. Figure 8.2 shows one side of the chart. Be sure to display this chart prominently at a level easily reached by your child.

Set Goals

The next step is to set goals. The first goal should be two weeks with no thumb-sucking, and the second goal should be six weeks with no thumb-sucking. The final goal should remain open-ended, for it will be achieved when your child no longer sucks during sleep. Although the daytime habit begins to be broken down in only a week, it takes approximately three months for a young child to break the nighttime habit completely. Treatment of the nighttime thumb-sucking habit will be discussed in Chapter 9.

Create a Contract

Once the charts are made and the goals are set, you and your child are ready to create a contract so that rules for reaching the goals are clearly outlined and understood. If he doesn't yet read, use a combination of simple words and pictures to create the contract. However you create the contract, state the goals and rules precisely. If you both know exactly what the rules are and adhere to them, you will avoid the arguments and tension that uncertainty brings.

Sometimes it helps if a third party sets the rules. A professional influence can be especially helpful in this area because, as we pointed out in Chapter 7, children are more

Thumbs Down For A...
Happy, Healthy Smile

1st Week	2nd Week	3rd Week	4th Week	5th Week	6th Week

I Can Do It! Yes, I Can!

Figure 8.2. One Side of Three-Month Progress Chart

likely to abide by the rules of a non-familiar third party. In addition, a third party relieves the parent of having to play the role of monitor. And when it's time to enforce the rules, you can blame it all on the third party: "You know the therapist said you can't put a sticker on your chart if you deliberately suck your thumb." And that's that! Figure 8.3 provides a sample contract that you may want to use to clearly state the goals.

Give Rewards

Rewards are positive reinforcements. Your child should receive a reward after each goal is achieved. Small rewards can be given for good progress during the first few days or week. These initial rewards are particularly valuable for younger children, who need more immediate gratification. Place a few small objects such as crayons, barrettes, matchbox cars, a certificate granting the child a special privilege—such as staying up a little later on a weekend night or a trip to the ice-cream store—in a grab bag. Let him pick one article or certificate after the first day without sucking; then every other day for the first week.

The rewards you give to your child when he reaches the two-week, six-week, and final goals should be determined by you, not by him. This is because the element of surprise makes it more fun, which increases his motivation and determination. These rewards could be special privileges, a toy, or an outing.

Do not think that rewards are bribes. Children working on the difficult task of eliminating a sucking habit deserve some tangible recognition for their accomplishment. This is particularly true of young children, who have a hard time appreciating the real value of giving up this behavior. They will need external compensation to maintain their determination, and they are entitled to it!

Make it a point to have the reward ready to present to

Thumb Contract

MOM & DAD ARE GOING TO GIVE ME THREE
SPECIAL SURPRISES FOR "KICKING" MY
THUMB HABIT AWAY!

The 1st surprise will be given to me when I have
14 days (2 weeks) in a row with NO sucking ALL day
and NO sucking ALL night.

The 2nd surprise will be given to me when I have 42
days (6 weeks) in a row with NO sucking ALL day
and NO sucking ALL night.

The 3rd surprise will be given to me when my
SLEEPY HABIT IS ALL GONE!

If I deliberately suck my thumb, I have to start
counting the days ALL OVER... FROM DAY ONE!

Signed_____

Mom & Dad_____

MY SMILE IS SPECIAL!
I CAN DO IT! YES, I CAN!

Figure 8.3. A Parent-Child Contract

your youngster on the very day that he achieves each goal. If you tell him that you "just haven't had a chance to get the reward yet," he will be very disheartened and will feel that his efforts to discontinue the sucking habit are not valued. The sucking behavior may start all over again. It is very important to give the prize on the day it is due. It is equally important to make the presentation a very special event!

Rewards can also come in the form of praise. When you notice that your child is doing something in order to stop himself from thumb-sucking, praise him. For example, if you see him holding his hands under his legs in an effort to avoid giving in to the sucking urge, let him know how proud you are that he is trying so hard. It is also helpful to let your child hear you speak positively to other people about his efforts. Fortunately, most young children don't mind if people outside the family know that they're working on getting rid of a thumb-sucking habit. In fact, they are often eager to tell the world about their efforts. Many little ones I work with take their charts to school for show-and-tell!

The more positive feedback your child receives for his efforts, the better it is for him. It will build his self-esteem and strengthen his resolve to get rid of the habit. When a goal is reached, have the whole family applaud the child, bake a cake to celebrate, or send him a letter. Children love to get mail, even if they can't read. Little notes commending the child's effort from grandparents or other relatives and friends are very helpful. If he can read, write special notes about the great job he is doing, and put them in various places, such as in his lunch bag or on his pillow before bedtime. All the positive reinforcement and approval will give your child a sense of personal pride, and soon the inner warmth of these good feelings will become the motivating force.

HOW CAN YOU HELP YOUR CHILD
STAY ON COURSE?

With all your hard work and determination, there is always the possibility that there will be setbacks. If you handle them properly, they will be temporary, and your child will be successful in breaking his habit.

Stick With the Contract

Remember that once you and your child have begun the program, there is no room for negotiation. All children will try to test the rules, but there must be a consequence for deliberate sucking behavior. Some parents are so eager to have their child stop the sucking that they overlook deliberate sucking lapses and rationalize that the youngster is doing better, or not sucking as often. If you give your child a prize under these circumstances, you will be reinforcing the wrong behavior. Consequently, he will not accomplish his goals, and he may become bored, frustrated, and reluctant to persevere. Therefore, he should not be allowed to put a sticker on his chart or receive a reward if there has been a deliberate sucking lapse. Furthermore, if there is an intentional slip, he must start counting progress from day one! Adherence to this rule will quickly teach your child that he must master self-control.

Don't Get Angry If Your Child Lapses

Keeping your cool is always the surest path to success. You should never respond to your child's deliberate slip by admonishing him. For instance, if you say, "What's the matter with you? Why can't you keep that thumb out of your mouth?" you're imposing your adult will on your child. This type of message makes him feel inadequate, lowers his self-esteem, and creates conflict between you. Your child will have lost an ally and he will feel like a failure, which may cause him to give up entirely.

Respond with empathy if your child should slip up. Put your arm around him and try to determine what the circumstances were when he had the lapse. Offer insight into the problem that stimulated the sucking response and lots of sympathy. For example, say to your youngster, "I know it's very hard to stop sucking, especially when you're tired and upset about something." Then ask him if he remembers why it's important to get rid of the sucking habit. It is not uncommon for young children to forget why they are trying to quit sucking.

A positive approach lets the youngster know that you love him unconditionally and that your love has nothing to do with his success in eliminating the sucking behavior. But the decision to continue or not to continue thumbsucking must be the child's. Children generally appreciate a patient, caring regard for their needs and are very likely to want to please you and keep trying.

Don't Worry if Your Child Is Not Ready to Stop

If your child has tried to stop and has had a number of deliberate sucking lapses, do not insist that he continue a program of elimination. The fact is, he is not able to discontinue the sucking activity *at this particular time*. The most positive thing you can do at this point is to tell your child that you know how important it is to pick just the right time to work on getting rid of the habit; and maybe now is not the right time. Then, simply drop the subject. You have nothing to lose and everything to gain. This approach lets your child off the hook, allows him to save face, and it keeps the door open. It is the best way to motivate your youngster to come to you in a few days, weeks, or months expressing a desire to address his habit seriously.

Use a Daytime Reminder

Because children with sucking habits are frequently unaware of their sucking activity, having something on the thumb to remind them when the activity occurs is a big help. The most effective reminder is an adhesive bandage. Bandages work well during the day; and young children usually enjoy wearing them, especially if they can pick out their favorite character-bandages for the project. I introduce this daytime reminder by telling children that we need special helpers to let them know when their thumb is trying to get into their mouth! By suggesting that the thumb has a mind of its own, the blame for sucking can be separated from the child. The thumb did it!

Children generally need assistance placing the adhesive bandage on their thumb, which should be placed comfortably around the top part of the thumb, above the first knuckle. If you tried doing this in the past and your child still sucked, place a bandage over the top of the thumb so that no skin is exposed, and then place a second bandage around the first.

The bandage introduces a different taste and feel, which are cues to remind the child that his thumb is in his mouth. You should be observant, but you should not panic or warn your child when you notice the thumb heading toward his mouth. If the habit is to be eliminated, your child must make a conscious choice not to suck. If he withdraws the thumb from his mouth as soon as he notices it, praise him, for it was not a deliberate lapse.

Some children cannot tolerate the bandages, and choose to have the bad-tasting liquid painted on the thumb. Other children would rather have no reminder at all. You can be flexible in this area. Remember that it is your child's decision. If he refuses to wear a reminder and has a slip that lasts more than a few seconds, there should be no sticker on the chart, and it's back to day one!

If your child does not suck at school or at daycare, it is not necessary for him to wear the bandages in these settings. However, many children start sucking as soon as they get in the car for the ride home from school. Therefore, it will be important to get the reminder on as soon as possible after school to avoid an unintentional slip. Rather than bothering with adhesive bandages in the car, it may be easier to keep a glove in the car.

Children who thumb-suck while they are at daycare or school will need extra bandages to take along in case the one they are wearing comes off. Speak to your child's teacher and enlist her help. Most teachers are eager to help and will follow your instructions in regard to replacing lost bandages. Ask teachers and aides *not* to enforce the wearing of the bandages or remind the child if they observe sucking activity, but to keep you informed of any lapses and their circumstances.

During the early stages of habit elimination, sucking can occur unintentionally simply because the reminder is not on the thumb. Children frequently have an inadvertent lapse just after a bath, especially in the evening when they are tired. After your child's bath, immediately dry the favorite thumb and replace the reminder.

There is a fine line between helping the child who truly wants to stop sucking and taking full responsibility for his success. Although parents can help their youngster replace a bandage, it is not their responsibility to enforce the wearing of a reminder. If children are allowed to be responsible for their own adhesive strip, it teaches them that they have a choice, that they are in control, and that the habit is their own responsibility. And, best of all, they learn that their parents have faith in their capabilities. Remember that behavior controlled by an outside force usually lasts only as long as the force is present.

When to Discontinue the Daytime Reminder

When you no longer see your child's thumb going toward his mouth during the day, it is probably safe to begin gradual elimination of the daytime reminder. To be on the safe side, it is a good idea to continue using it during the evening when your child is tired or watching television.

Be Mindful Without Being Intrusive

If accidental sucking lapses are counted as deliberate, children quickly give up because they become frustrated and conclude that they are not able to control the behavior. In addition, if they have frequent lapses because of parental inconsistency, they may give up for the same reason. Children cannot imagine that their parents are capable of making a mistake. Instead, they hold themselves responsible. You must be watchful without being intrusive; and be extra careful in those situations in which the sucking occurs or when the reminder could accidentally come off.

Keep Your Child Busy

Plan a variety of activities to distract your youngster from the thumb-sucking behavior. Activities that keep his hands occupied, such as drawing, coloring, puzzles, crafts, and games, are especially helpful. If the hands are busy, the thumb will not be going to the mouth. Remember to limit television viewing, especially during the first two weeks.

Each hour and each day that goes by without sucking breaks down the cycle of the habit, and your child will begin to feel more comfortable, confident, and determined. Before you know it, usually after the first week of total withdrawal, the motion of the thumb going to the mouth will be absent or minimal during the day. You will see your child beaming with pride—particularly if you notice, encourage, and praise his efforts *frequently*. The following suggestions will be of help:

- If the mouth is busy; the thumb will not try to get into it! Allow your child to chew on sugarless gum; and have ready supplies of fruit, carrot sticks, celery, or popcorn. This is especially helpful during those times when thumb-sucking commonly occurs—TV time, riding in the car, and when your child is hungry, fatigued, or stressed. Avoid gum or other sugarless products that contain the natural sweetener *sorbitol*, for it can cause gas, stomach pain, and diarrhea. Furthermore, don't give your child caffeine products, because they can cause hyperactivity, irritability, and difficulty in falling asleep.

- Get an unbreakable container with a lid and straw and fill it with juice or water. Let your child keep it handy, especially during the first few difficult days, and encourage him to take a sip when he is having a strong urge to suck.

- Make toys and collages out of egg cartons, paper-towel tubes, plastic bottles, yarn, buttons, ribbon, wrapping paper. Use your imagination!

- Children love to help cook, especially if it's something really tasty. Mix up a big batch of cookie dough together!

- Pitch a tent in the back yard and sleep under the stars.

- Get out the volleyball, croquet set, or plastic swimming pool.

- Visit a children's museum, planetarium, aquarium, or zoo.

The possibilities are limitless. Whatever you decide to do, make it easy and enjoyable. And remember to tell your youngster often how proud your are of him for working so hard to eliminate the thumb-sucking habit.

CONCLUSION

You are on your way. Positive behavior modification is an excellent tool for the elimination of destructive habits. The system of rewards is positive and non-threatening, and it encourages children to keep going when they are struggling against a very strong desire to thumb-suck. And, best of all, everyone comes out a winner because it is non-accusatory, and it unites children and parents who are trying to achieve a common goal.

Chapter 9

ELIMINATING THE NIGHTTIME SUCKING HABIT

T he subconscious sucking activity at bedtime is prevalent in all children with a thumb-sucking habit. It is
the most persistent aspect of the thumb-sucking
habit and the most difficult to eliminate. Children suck
before falling asleep and intermittently throughout the
sleep cycle.

WHY IS THE NIGHTTIME HABIT
DIFFICULT TO BREAK?

The nighttime habit is difficult to break because we are not
conscious of our behavior while we are sleeping. During
REM sleep—the deepest stage of the sleep cycle—physical
movement is limited, and so there is minimal sucking
activity. However, we also have periods of light sleep. During light sleep, the child may turn over, pull the covers up,
and resume sucking, which gradually returns her to deep
sleep. But a child who is trying not to suck may fully
awaken because she becomes conscious of the fact that

she has to control something that had been automatic behavior.

WHAT NIGHTTIME RITUAL
SHOULD PARENTS ESTABLISH?

In order to ensure that the nighttime thumb-sucking habit
will be completely eliminated, you should take extra pre-
cautions before you put your child to bed. Remember that
no matter how busy or tired you are, the time you spend
with your child now is the surest, fastest way to success.
And, best of all, it will bring you and your child closer
together.

Make Bedtime Comforting

A child with a sucking habit must learn how to fall asleep
without the comfort of her thumb. Allow enough time at
bedtime, especially for the first few nights, to make this an
easier transition for your child. Your aim is to make the
bedtime ritual comforting and personal. Your efforts will
let your child know that you are with her in her struggle
to discontinue the sucking habit.

What to Avoid Before Bedtime

Your child should be in a relaxed state before beginning
the nighttime ritual. For this reason, the two-hour period
preceding bedtime must not be over-stimulating. That
means no roughhousing, excessive exercise, arguments, or
upsetting television programs.

What to Do Before Bedtime

There are various ways to relax that will make falling
asleep much easier. First, a bath, especially a bubble bath,
is fun for children. It also signals the end of the day, which

helps get them psychologically ready to go to sleep. A light snack consisting of some type of milk product can be helpful in bringing on sleep. During the first week, let your child suck on a sugarless mint just before bedtime. After snacking and brushing her teeth, your child can climb into bed and listen to a story. And when it's time for lights out, soft music or a relaxation tape can be extremely helpful.

If your child is still having difficulty, try a little back rub or lie down with her for a little while until she starts to drift off. Remember, the first week or so is going to be very difficult for your child. For years, she has been depending on her thumb to help her fall asleep. Now she will need your support as she learns to fall asleep without thumb-sucking. If you find it necessary to lie down with your child for the first few nights, gradually decrease the amount of time that you spend with her each night. For instance, on the first night, you might have to stay until she falls asleep. After that, set a time limit of ten or twenty minutes. But tell your child that you will be back in fifteen minutes to check on her. Be sure you follow through and check in fifteen minutes; if she's still awake, offer brief comfort and leave the room again. Repeat the sequence until your child is asleep. This routine will reassure her that you have not abandoned her in her effort to fall asleep without sucking.

Use a Nighttime Reminder

Before introducing the nighttime reminder to prevent the sucking activity, explain to your child that she doesn't know what she is doing during her sleep. Tell her that many times when you check on her during the night, her thumb has sneaked into her mouth, and that you are going to make a sleep-time puppet to help her out.

The sleep-time puppet can be made out of a long cotton

tube sock. Let your child help create a happy-face character with permanent nontoxic markers or fabric paints. Most young children delight in this approach to help them discontinue their nighttime sucking habit, and they embrace this hand puppet as a new friend. You can use the puppets in Figure 9.1 as a guide.

The sock should be worn whenever your child sleeps, including during naptime. Be sure to fasten it securely or sew it to her pajama top or T-shirt.

If your child naps at daycare, make an extra puppet, and leave it at the daycare center. Young children love their sleep-time hand puppets. One mother told me that several of her child's friends at daycare showed up with a puppet sock of their own for naptime, even though they had no sucking habits! Younger siblings frequently want a puppet of their own, too! Be prepared to make more than one.

As an extra precaution, have your child wear an adhesive bandage under the sock. Children usually take the sock off in the morning before going to the bathroom, and they may forget to put a bandage on before beginning the day. This may cause her to suck unintentionally, which can make her extremely discouraged. Remember that children usually view any lapse as a failure.

HOW CAN YOU BE SURE THE HABIT IS OVER?

If your child has been wearing the bedtime reminder for three consecutive months, and you see no signs of sucking activity during the day, you can test to see if the habit is finished. Before your child goes to bed, place a piece of cotton on top of her thumb and then place a cloth adhesive bandage over the top of the cotton leaving a little cotton exposed on each side of the bandage. Place a second bandage around the base of the first one.

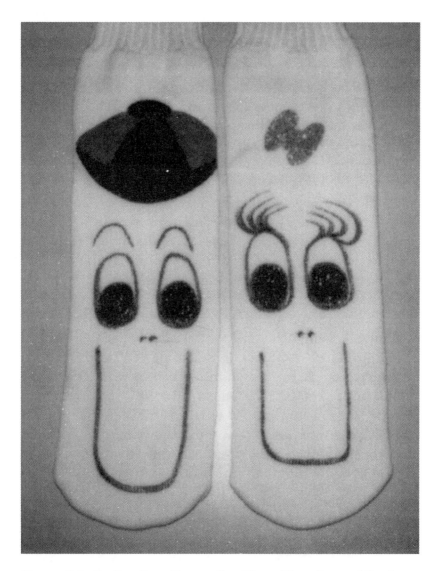

Figure 9.1. Smiley Sam/Samantha Sleep-Time Puppet Socks

Then, have your child use a disclosing tablet—the little red tablets used to reveal plaque left on the teeth after brushing works well. Tell her to let the tablet dissolve in her mouth—you don't want her to swallow it—and spit out the excess when she's finished. The idea is to coat the mouth with the red coloring, so do not allow her to drink anything or rinse her mouth! Of course, your youngster will go to bed with a pink mouth, and if the subconscious habit is still present, the tape and cotton will be pink and wet in the morning. If this happens, it is extremely important that you be very positive. Simply have your child continue to wear the sock for a few more weeks, and then test again.

Do the test when your child is at home in her own environment and when she will have a normal bedtime. Before she goes to sleep, remind your child that she should not feel bad if the thumb slips into her mouth during the test, because she doesn't know what the thumb is doing when she is sleeping. It simply means that the sleepy mind has not yet forgotten about the thumb-sucking habit, and she will need her nighttime helper a while longer.

If there is no evidence of sucking, your child can go without the sock, but she should continue to wear a single cloth bandage to bed. I suggest that the test be repeated two or three more times at one or two week intervals. If your child continues to test without evidence of sucking, and you are not observing any sucking during sleep, she can go to bed without anything on the thumb.

What if There Is a Relapse?

Occasionally a child will go for several months with no problems; and then, after an extremely stressful day, she might slip up and start sucking during sleep. If sucking is observed, be positive! Do not make an issue of the unintentional slip. Continue checking to see if the activity takes place for several consecutive nights. If so, this may be an indication that there is something upsetting going on in the child's life. If you are not aware of any particular cause of stress at home, you may want to visit your youngster's school to evaluate whether she is having a problem there.

Your child is likely to be upset about this lapse, especially if the nighttime reminders have not been in use for awhile. But to prevent re-establishment of the habit, it will be necessary to return to the bedtime helpers. Explain to your child that you observed the sucking activity while she was sleeping and assure her that you know it was not deliberate. Tell her how proud you are of her for having done so much to get rid of her habit, but it will be a little longer before she can go to bed without her bandage or puppet. You can retest when you think the time is appropriate.

CONCLUSION

Remember that the nighttime habit will usually take much longer to conquer than the daytime habit. The important thing is to be consistent, positive, and patient in your efforts to help your child. If you make the nighttime ritual fun for your child, if you treat her thumb as though it is separate from her, and if you respond to any lapses with empathy and understanding, it will ensure your youngster's success in overcoming the thumb-sucking habit once and for all.

CONCLUSION

M y life has been truly blessed because of my work with the precious innocence and unconditional trust of the children who have come under my care. Equally satisfying is the knowledge that I have helped thousands of families overcome a problem that was a significant source of frustration and anxiety. It is my hope that this book will help thousands of other children and parents.

You now have a thorough understanding of the nature of the thumb-sucking behavior and the wide variety of circumstances that affect, stimulate, and prolong the activity. And you have learned how to treat the problem with comprehensive, kind techniques based on sound principles of child development. Indeed, the philosophy of kindness, respect, and understanding can be applied to all aspects of child rearing.

It is truly impossible to describe the joy of watching children discover the inner strength to overcome this behavior and free themselves from the bondage of feeling inadequate or flawed; no longer subjected to chronic emotional pain and cruel responses from others as a result of their sucking activity. It is equally joyous to watch their parents, who rejoice and reclaim a close and meaningful relationship with their youngsters because they have come together to achieve a common goal in a compassionate and positive way.

You too will revel in the joy of watching your child triumph and grow from this experience. It will enrich your child and your relationship with your child. Be prepared to watch your youngster go forward unencumbered, free to explore the world with an enhanced self-image and inner peace.

BIBLIOGRAPHY

Baalack, L. B., and Frisk, A. K. "Finger Sucking in Children: A Study of Incidence and Occlusal Conditions." *Odontologica Scandinavica.* 29:499. 1971.

Bloem, J. J. A., Kon, M., and de Graaf, F. H. "Rotational Deformity of the Index Finger Caused by Reversed Finger Sucking." *Annals of Plastic Surgery.* 21. 1988.

Bosma, J. "Physiology of the Mouth, Pharynx, and Esophagus." In Paparella, N. M. and Shumrich, D. A., editors: *Otolaryngology.* Philadelphia: W. B. Saunders Co. 1973.

Brazelton, T. B. "Implications of Infant Development Among the Mayan Indians of Mexico." In Leiderman, P. H., Tulkin, S. R. and Rosenfeld, A. *Culture and Infancy.* New York: Academic Press Inc. 151–87. 1977.

Campbell-Reid, D. A., and Price, A. H. K. "Digital Deformities and Dental Malocclusion Due To Finger Sucking." *British Journal of Plastic Surgery.* 37:445–52. 1984.

Christensen, A. P., and Sanders, M. R. "Habit Reversal and Differential Reinforcement of Other Behavior in the

Treatment of Thumb Sucking: An Analysis of Generalization and Side-Effects." *Journal of Child Psychology and Psychiatry and Allied Disciplines.* 28(2): 281–95. 1987.

Corrucini, R. S., and Potter, R. H. Y. "Genetic Analysis of Occlusal Variation in Twins." *American Journal of Orthodontics.* 78: 140–54. 1980.

Day, A. J. W, and Foster, T. D. "An Investigation Into the Prevalence of Molar Crossbite and Some Associated Aetiological Conditions." *British Society of the Study of Orthodontics.* 57:18. 1970–71.

Dion, D., Berscheid, E., and Walster, E. "What Is Beautiful Is Good." *Journal of Personality and Social Psychology.* 24: 285–90. 1972.

Eisenbaum, I. W. "A Correlation of Traumatized Anterior Teeth to Occlusion." *Journal of Dentistry for Children.* 30:229. 1963

Erikson, E. *Childhood and Society.* New York: W. W. Norton, 1963.

Flavell, J. H. *The Developmental Psychology of Jean Piaget.* New York: Van Nostrand Reinhold, 1963.

Fletcher, B. T. "Etiology of Finger Sucking: Review of Literature." *ASCD Journal of Dentistry for Children.* 42:293–8. 1975.

Fletcher, S. G., Casteel, R. L., and Bradley, D. P. "Tongue Thrust Swallow, Speech Articulation, and Age." *Journal of Speech and Hearing Disorders.* 26:201–8. 1961.

Frantz, D. "Apical Root Resorption in the Anterior Open Bite Malocclusion." Master's thesis, University of Washington, 1965.

Friman, P. C. and Schmitt, B. D. "Thumb Sucking: Pediatricians' Guidelines." *Clinical Pediatrics.* 28 (10): 438–40. 1989.

Gordon, T. *P.E.T. Parent Effectiveness Training,* Revised Edition. New York: New American Library, 1990.

Graber, L. W. "Psychological Considerations of Orthodontic Treatment." In *Psychological Aspects of Facial Form, Center for Human Growth and Development.* University of Michigan, Ann Arbor, Michigan: 81–119. 1981.

Graber, T. M. "Thumb and Finger Sucking." *American Journal of Orthodontics.* 45:259–64. 1959.

Hanson, M. L., and Barrett, R. H. *Fundamentals of Orofacial Myology.* Springfield, IL: Charles C. Thomas, 1988.

Hanson, M. L., and Cohen, M. S. "Effects of Form and Function on Swallowing and the Developing Dentition." *American Journal of Orthodontics,* 72:63–82. 1973.

Herd, J. R. "Apical Tooth Root Resorption." *Austin Dental Journal.* 16:269–74. 1971.

Honzik, M. P. and Mckee, J. P. "The Sex Difference in Thumb-Sucking." *Journal of Pediatrics.* 61:726–32. 1962.

Hughes, J., Smith, T. W., Kosterlitz, H. W., Fothergill, L. A., Morgan, B. A., and Morris, H. R. "Identification of Two Related Pentapeptides From the Brain With Potent Opiate Agonist Activity." *Nature.* 258 (5536):577–9. 1975.

Humphrey, T. "The Development of Mouth Opening and Related Reflexes Involving the Oral Area of Human Fetuses. *Alabama Journal of Medical Science.* 5:126–157. 1968.

Illingworth, R. S. *The Normal Child.* New York: Churchill Livingston Inc., 1987.

Infante, P. F. "An Epidemiologic Study of Finger Habits in Preschool Children, As Related to Malocclusion, Socio-economic Status, Race, Sex and Size of Community." *Journal of Dentistry for Children.* 43:33–38. 1976.

Ingervall, B., Mohlin, B., and Thilander, B. "Prevalence of Symptoms of Functional Disturbances of the Masticatory System in Swedish Men." *Journal of Oral Rehabilitation.* 7:185–97. 1980.

Jenny, J. "A Social Perspective on Need and Demand for Orthodontic Treatment." *International Dental Journal.* 25:248–56. 1975

Johnson, E. D. and Larson, B. E. "Thumb-Sucking: Classification and Treatment." *Journal of Dentistry for Children.* 60(4):392–8. 1993.

Kellum, G. D., Gross, A.M., Hale, S.T., Eiland, S., and Williams, C. "Thumbsucking as Related to Placement and Acoustic Aspects of /S,Z/ and Lingual Rest Postures." *International Journal of Orofacial Myology.* 20:4–9. 1994.

Kelly, J. E., Sanchez, M., and Van Kirk, L. E. "An Assessment of the Occlusion of the Teeth of Children." National Center for Health Statistics, U.S. Public Health Service, DHEW Publication No. (HRA) 74-1612, Washington, D.C., Pg. 11. 1973.

Knott, V. B. and O'Meara, W. F. "Serial Data on Primary Incisor Root Resorption and Gingival Emergence of Permanent Successors." *Angle Orthodontist.* 37:212–22. 1967.

Kohler, L. and Hoist, K. "Malocclusion and Sucking Habits of Four-Year-Old Children." *Acta Paediatric Scandinavia.* 62:1–7. 1973.

Kolata, G. B. "!Kung Hunter-Gatherers: Feminism, Diet, and Birth Control." *Science.* 185:932–5. 1974.

Konner, M. "Infancy Among the Kalahari Desert San." In Leiderman, P. H., Tulkin, S. R. and Rosenfeld, A., editors. *Culture and Infancy.* New York: Academic Press, Inc. 287–328. 1977.

Konner, M. "Behavior Development." In Leiderman, P. H., Tulkin, S. R. and Rosenfeld, A., editors. *Culture and Infancy.* New York: Academic Press, Inc. 90–109. 1977.

Konner, M. and Worthman, C. "Nursing Frequency, Gonadal Function, and Birth Spacing among !Kung Hunter-Gatherers." *Science.* 201:788–91. 1980.

Larsson, E. In Larsson, E. "Artificial Sucking Habits: Prevalence and Effect on Occlusion." *International Journal of Orofacial Myology.* 20:10–21. 1994.

Larsson, E. F. and Dahlin, K. G. "The Prevalence and Etiology of the Initial Dummy- and Finger-Sucking Habit." *American Journal of Orthodontia.* 87:432–5. 1985.

Linge, B. O. and Linge, O. "Apical Root Resorption in Upper Anterior Teeth." *European Journal of Orthodontics.* 5:178–83. 1983.

Lundstrom, A. "Nature vs. Nurture in Dentofacial Variation." *European Journal of Orthodontics.* 6:77–91. 1984.

Madhok, R. "Finger Sucking-An Unhealthy Habit?" *Midwife-Health Visit Community Nurse.* 25(11):482–3. 1989.

Mason, R. M. "Orthodontic Perspectives On Orofacial Myofunctional Therapy." *International Journal of Orofacial Myology.* 14(1):49–55. 1988.

Massler, M. and Perrault, J. "Root Resorption in the Permanent Teeth of Young Adults." *Journal of Dentistry for Children.* 21:158–64. 1954.

Milkman, H. B. and Sunderwirth, S. G. *Craving For Ecstasy, The Consciousness & Chemistry of Escape.* Toronto: Lexington Books, 1987.

Milne, I., and Cleall, J. "Cinefluorographic Study of Functional Adaptation of the Oropharyngeal Structures." *Angle Orthodontist.* 40:267–83. 1970.

Modeer, T., Odenrick, L., and Lindner, A. "Sucking Habits and Their Relation to Posterior Crossbite in 4-Year-Old Children." *Scandinavian Journal of Dental Research.* 90: 323–8. 1982.

Morris, A. L. et al. *Seriously Handicapping Orthodontic Conditions.* Washington, D.C.: National Academy of Sciences, 1977.

Moyers, R. *Handbook of Orthodontics.* Chicago: Year Book Medical Publishers, 1973.

Newman, W. G. "Possible Etiologic Factors in External Root Resorption." *American Journal of Orthodontics.* 67(5): 522–39. 1975.

Nord, F. L. "Reader Comments." *Journal of the American Dental Association.* 64:872–3. 1962.

Ogarrd, B., Larsson, E. and Lindsten, R. "The Effect of Sucking Habits, Cohort, Sex, Intercanine Arch Widths, and Breast or Bottle Feeding on Posterior Crossbite in Norwegian and Swedish 3-Year-Old Children." *American Journal of Orthodontics and Dentofacial Orthopedics.* 106(2): 161–6. 1994.

Passman, R. H., Halonen, J. S. "A Developmental Survey of Young Children's Attachments to Inanimate Objects." *Journal Genetic Psychology.* 134:165–178. 1979.

Popovich, F., Thompson, G. W. "Thumb- and Finger-Sucking: Its Relation to Malocclusion." *American Journal of Orthodontics.* 63:148–55. 1973

Profitt, W. R. *Contemporary Orthodontics.* St. Louis: C.V. Mosby. 1986.

Rankin, E. A., Jabaley, M. E., Blair, S. J., and Fraser, K. D. "Acquired Rotational Digital Deformity in Children As a Result of Finger Sucking." *Journal of Hand Surgery.* 13A(4). 1988.

Roberts, J. and Baird, J. T. *Parent Ratings of Behavioral Patterns of Children.* Department of Health, Education and Welfare, No. (HS) 72–1010, 1971.

Rogers, J. H. "Swallowing Patterns of a Normal-Population Sample Compared to Those of Patients From an Orthodontic Practice." *American Journal of Orthodontics.* 47:647–89. 1961.

Rubel, I. "Atypical Root Resorption of Maxillary Primary Central Incisors Due to Digital Sucking: A Report of 82 Cases." *Journal of Dentistry for Children.* 53:201–4. 1986.

Shaw, W. C. "The Influence of Children's Dentofacial Appearance on their Social Attractiveness as Judged by Peers and Lay Adults." *American Journal of Orthodontics.* 79:399–413. 1981.

Shostak, M. A. "!Kung Woman's Memories of Childhood." In Lee, R. B., and DeVore, I., editors. *Kalahari Hunter-Gatherers.* Cambridge: Harvard University Press, 246–78. 1976.

Skakun, B. "Who Needs Valium? A Thumb Is Free and Always Handy." *Wall Street Journal.* Monday, August 4, 1986.

Stewart, R., Barber, T., Troutman, K., and Wei S.H.Y. *Pediatric Dentistry.* St. Louis: C. V. Mosby, 1982.

Stone, O. J., and Mullens, J. F. "Chronic Paronychnia in Children." *Clinical Pediatrics.* Philadelphia. 2:104. 1976

Straub, W. J. "Malfunction of the Tongue." *American Journal of Orthodontia.* 46:404–24. 1960.

Stricker, G., Clifford, E., Cohen, L. K., Giddon, D. B., Meskin, L. H., and Evan, C. A. "Psychosocial Aspects of Craniofacial Disfigurement." *American Journal of Orthodontics.* 76:410–22. 1979.

Taylor, M., and Peterson, D. "Effect of Digit-Sucking Habits on Root Morphology in Primary Incisors." *American Journal of Pediatric Dentistry.* 5:62–3. 1983.

Traisman, A. S., Traisman, H. S. "Thumb and Finger Sucking: A Study of 2,650 Infants and Children." *Journal of Pediatrics.* 53:566–72. 1958.

Turbeville, A. F. and Fearnow, R. G. "Is It Possible to Identify the Child Who Is a 'High Risk' Candidate for the Accidental Ingestion of Poison?" *Clinical Pediatrics.* 15: 918–19. 1976.

Werlich, E. *The Prevalence of Variant Swallowing Patterns in a Group of Seattle School Children.* Master's Thesis. University of Washington, 1962.

Wright, L., Schaefer, A. G. and Solomons, G. *Encyclopedia of Pediatric Psychology.* Baltimore: University Park Press, 1979.

SUGGESTED READINGS

Infant Care and Emotional and Physical Development

Brazelton, T. Berry. *Touchpoints: The Essential Reference: Your Child's Emotional and Behavioral Development.* New York: Addison Wesley, 1996.

Briggs, Dorothy Corkille. *Your Child's Self-Esteem: The Key to Life.* New York: Dolphin Books, 1975.

Driscoll, Jeanne Watson and Walker, Marsha. *Taking Care of Your New Baby: A Guide to Infant Care.* Garden City Park, NY: Avery Publishing Group, 1996.

Goleman, Daniel. *Emotional Intelligence.* New York: Bantam Books, 1997.

Hill, Barbara Albers. *Baby Tactics: Parenting Tips That Really Work.* Garden City Park, NY: Avery Publishing Group, 1991.

Ilg, Frances L., Ames, Louise Bates, Baker, Sidney M. *Child Behavior: The Classic Child Care Manual From Gesell Institute of Human Development.* New York: Harper Perennial, 1992.

Leach, Penelope. *Your Growing Child: From Babyhood Through Adolescence.* New York: Alfred A. Knopf, 1996.

Leach, Penelope. *Your Baby & Child: From Birth to Age Five.* New York: Alfred A. Knopf, 1997.

Sears, William. *Keys to Calming the Fussy Baby.* New York: Barron's Parenting Keys Educational Series, 1991.

Spock, Benjamin and Rothenberg, Michael B. *Dr. Spock's Baby and Child Care,* Revised Pocket Edition. New York: Pocket Books, 1992.

Family Communication and Discipline

Covey, Stephen R. The Seven Habits of Highly Effective Families: Building a Beautiful Family Culture in a Turbulent World. New York: Golden Books: 1997.

Dobson, James C. *Parenting Isn't for Cowards.* Dallas, TX: Word, 1987.

Dobson, James C. *The New Dare to Discipline,* Revised Edition. Wheaton, IL: Tyndale House, 1992.

Faber, Adele and Mazlish, Elaine. *How to Talk So Kids Will Listen and Listen So Kids Will Talk.* New York: Avon Books, 1991.

Gordon, Thomas. *P.E.T. Parent Effectiveness Training,* Revised Edition. New York: New American Library, 1990.

Seligman, Martin, Reivich, Karen, Jaycox, Lisa and Gillham, Jane. *The Optimistic Child.* New York: Harperperennial, 1996.

Sprinkle, Patricia. *Children Who Do Too Little, Why Your Kids Need to Work Around the House (And How to Get Them to Do It).* Grand Rapids, MI: Zondervan Publishing House, 1996.

Windell, James. *Children Who Say No When You Want Them to Say Yes: Failsafe Discipline Strategies for Stubborn and Oppositional Children and Teens.* New York: Macmillan General References, 1996.

Siblings

Dunn, Judy. *From One Child to Two: What to Expect, How to Cope and How to Enjoy Your Growing Family.* New York: Fawcett Books, 1995.

Faber, Adele and Mazlish, Elaine. *Siblings Without Rivalry: How to Help Your Children Live Together So You Can Live Too.* New York: Avon Books, 1988.

Samalin, Nancy and Whitney, Catherine. *Loving Each One Best: A Caring and Practical Approach to Raising Siblings.* New York: Bantam Books, 1997.

Sleep Problems

Cuthbertson, Joanne and Schevill, Susie. *Helping Your Child Sleep Through the Night.* New York: Doubleday, 1985.

Ferber, Richard. *Solve Your Child's Sleep Problems.* New York: Fireside/Simon & Schuster, 1986.

Helping Children Cope With Divorce

Ahrons, Constance. The Good Divorce: Keeping Your Family Together When Your Marriage Comes Apart. New York: Basic Books, 1995.

Blau, Melinda. *Families Apart: Ten Keys to Successful Co-Parenting.* New York: Perigee, 1995.

Garrity, Carla B. and Baris, Mitchell A. *Caught in the Middle: Protecting the Children of High-Conflict Divorce.* San Francisco: Jossey-Bass Publishing, 1997.

Hart, Archibald. *Helping Children Survive Divorce: What to Expect; How to Help.* Dallas, TX: Word Publishing, 1997.

Marston, Stephanie. *The Divorced Parent: Successful Strategies for Raising Your Children After Separation.* New York: Pocket Books, 1995.

Schneider, Meg F. and Zuckerberg, Joan Offerman. *Difficult Questions Kids Ask and Are Too Afraid to Ask About Divorce.* New York: Fireside Books, 1996.

Work and Family

Bravo, Ellen. *The Job/Family Challenge: A 9 to 5 Guide.* New York: John Wiley & Sons, 1995.

Dacyczyn, Amy. *Tightwad Gazett III: Promoting Thrift As a Viable Alternative Lifestyle.* New York: Villard Books, 1997.

Peters, Joan K. *When Mothers Work: Loving Our Children Without Sacrificing Our Selves.* New York: Addison-Wesley Publishing, 1997.

Sal, June Solnit, Kollenberg, Kit, and Melinkoff, Ellen. *The Working Parents Handbook.* New York, 1996.

St. James, Elaine and Vera Cole. *Simplify Your Life With Kids: 100 Ways to Make Family Life Easier and More Fun.* Kansas City, *Andrews & McMeel, 1997.*

St. James, Elaine. *Living the Simple Life: A Guide to Scaling Down and Enjoying More.* New York: Hyperion, 1997.

Family Activities and Crafts

Better Homes and Gardens. *More Incredibly Awesome Crafts for Kids.* Des Moines, Iowa: Meredith Corporation/Better Homes and Gardens, 1997.

Disney. *Family Fun Crafts.* New York: Hyperion, 1997.

Perry, Susan K. and Chesman, Andrea. *Fun Time, Family Time.* New York: Avon Books, 1996.

Silberg, Jackie and Noll, Cheryl Kirk. *300 Three Minute Games: Quick and Easy Activities of 2–5 Year Olds.* New York: Gryphon House, 1997.

Solga, Kim and Hershberger, Priscilla. *Craft Fun: 92 Exciting, Original and Easy-to-Make Projects Kids Will Love to Do!* Cincinnati, OH: North Light Books, 1997.

Thomas, Dian. *Backyard Roughing it Easy: Unique Recipes for Outdoor Cooking, Plus Great Ideas for Creative Family Fun — All Just Steps from Your Back Door.* Cincinnati, OH: Betterway Publishing; 1997.

Weston, Denise Chapman and Weston, Mark. *Playwise: 365 Fun-Filled Activities for Building Character, Conscience and Emotional Intelligence in Children.* New York: Putnam, 1996.

INDEX